GW01605142

Happy Xmas

Elizabeth R

LORD GNOME OF THE RINGS

This modern classic tells the epic story of the small sturdy Gnome who sets out one bright day from the little hamlet of Neasden, on his search for gold. With him go his trusted companions–Strobes, the obsequious dwarf; Sue, Grabbit and Runne, his legal advisors, and beautiful fun-loving Rita Chevrolet (42-31-65), his travelling companion and confidante.

Ahead lie the gleaming Mountains of Money with their precious store of treasure. But many foes are lying in wait to harass the travellers. Writs and injunctions fly about Gnome's bruised and battered head as he struggles manfully onwards towards his last thrilling fight to the death with the evil dragon Goldsmaug.

Published in Great Britain by Private Eye Productions Ltd.,
34 Greek Street London W1.
In association with Andre Deutsch Ltd., 105 Great
Russell Street, London WC1.

SBN 233 96827 x

Designed by Peter Windett.

Printed by Feb Edge Litho, 3-4 The Oval, London E2 9DS

LORD GNOME OF THE RINGS

THE BEST OF

PRIVATE EYE

1976

A PRIVATE EYE BOOK WITH ANDRÉ DEUTSCH

FRANK MUIR welcomes you to the Gnome Trashy Book Club

"Fwankly, I was amazed by the fantastic value for money that Gnome Trashy Book Club gives.

3 books for 5p is not bad — when you think that a bottle of whiskey nowadays costs thirty quid!

You don't have to be a literary type to enjoy these wonderful books in the privacy of your own home.

Take a tip from Fwank. Invest in Gnome Trashy Book Club NOW."

Memo to Accts Dept: To being photographed with pipe against leather bound books; giving name to blurb compiled by your publicity dept; accepting lunch from B.D. Froth (Sales Manager) and listening to boring conversation of . . . . £8,000 + VAT

As a member you can SAVE 95% on the latest best-sellers like these!

THE OXFORD BOOK OF TELEPHONE NUMB...

THE RIDDLE OF THE WINDMILLS

VICTORIAN DYMCHURCH

REG BETJEMAN

MAKE YOUR OWN MATCHES

A.P. Rushton

A BOOK OF BATH TAPS

M.R. WHEATCROFT

1. A BOOK OF BATH TAPS
by M.R. Wheatcroft
This is not just a book for the specialist. Everyone, young and old, can enjoy its amusing and well-informed commentary on this fascinating topic. NORMAL PRICE £47.

2. VICTORIAN DYMCHURCH IN PHOTOGRAPHY
by Reg Betjeman (no relation)
A fascinating pictorial account of a bygone era. NORMAL PRICE £96.

3. THE OXFORD BOOK OF TELEPHONE NUMBERS
(Edited by Sir Mboto Carter-Ruck)
An invaluable reference book for specialist and non-specialist alike. NORMAL PRICE £172.

4. MAKE YOUR OWN MATCHES
by A.P. Rushton (fully illustrated)
An invaluable aid to enthusiasts and non-enthusiasts alike. NORMAL PRICE £76.

5. THE RIDDLE OF THE WINDMILLS
by Prof. Barry Mendelsohn.
Are windmills really Royal Tombs? Prof. Mendelsohn investigates this fascinating subject. NORMAL PRICE £106.

Neasditz!

Hauptmann Hildebrand von Wankel

Obergruppenfuhrer Spenz.

Kapitan Willi Barnetscnon.

It was nine o'clock. The chimes of the George V Memorial Hall in nearby FineFare Road woke Hauptmann Hildebrand von Wankel from a deep sleep.

"Mein Gott!" he exclaimed. "Look at ze time!"

There was a knock on the door and the friendly voice of Florrie Nabarro came from outside the "cell".

"Everybody decent?"

In two minutes von Wankel was washed, shaved and completely dressed in full uniform. Spenz and Barnetschon were already standing to attention beside their beds and had been since seven o'clock.

Florrie trundled a large tea trolley into the room.

"Poached eggs again for you, ducks?" She pinched Obergruppenfuhrer Spenz's cheek playfully.

The high-ranking German stiffened, beads of perspiration glistening on his bald pate.

"I vill get you for zis!" he hissed as the genial canteen lady poured him a steaming mug of tea.

"Get this down you, dearie. A nice cup of tea works wonders, that's what I always say."

Kapitan Willi Barnetschon could stand it no longer.

"Vill you plis address us by our proper military ranks. Enough of zis ducks and dearies, bitte, or I shall report you to ze Geneva Convention!"

As he spoke the Camp Commandant Lt.-Col. "Buffy" Betjeman shuffled into the "cell" wearing an old stained dressing gown and bedroom slippers.

'Gosh! That bacon smells good!" he beamed. "Mind if I join you?"

Barnetschon's nostrils quivered with suppressed rage. The veins on his neck stood out like taut wires. He could contain himself no longer.

"Vere is your uniform, Britisher pig?"

The Lieutenant Colonel seemed surprised.

"Uniform, old man? Oh, golly, there's no need to bother. No one does much. Only worn mine once. Don't you chaps spoil your breakfast worrying about uniforms. Gosh this toast is jolly tasty."

Before Barnetschon could reply the Commandant and Florrie wandered out, leaving the three prisoners in a mood of silent fury.

"Himmel!" von Wankel snarled. "Ve must escape from zis hell-hole as soon as possible! Ze next thing they vill be bringing us breakfast in bed!"

"Come on you naughty boys! Five more minutes to lights out now!"

Florrie Nabarro, the warm-hearted Neasditz char collected the three cocoa mugs that had been put in a neat row on the make-shift chest of drawers, and shuffled towards the door of Cell 94.

"Are you sure you don't want a hot water bottle, Mr Spenz?"

" 'Obergrgruppenfuhrer'! Pliss address me by my renk. All officers must be spoken to in accordance viz ze regulations B497 paragraph 4 Section C!"

Florrie gave a throaty chuckle.

"Cor! You're a card and no mistake!"

After she had gone Spenz, von Wankel and Barnetschon sprang from their beds and huddled over the blazing log fire.

"Listen," hissed Spenz, unrolling the large Ordnance Survey map which Col. 'Buffy' Betjeman had given them at their own request.

There was silence in the room. From below came the laughter of the Commandant as he listened to ITMA on the radio.

"Listen!" said Spenz again, pointing to the map. "Here is ze main gate. From my information zere are no guards here at any time of ze day or night."

"Gott in Himmel!" cried Barnetschon, his face flushed with anger. "Vot a hell-hole ve heff landed in!"

Von Wankel could hardly restrain himself.

"Zis Britisch vill stop at nozzing! Imagine! A camp viz no guards! Impossible!"

"Look for yourself, Hauptmann," shouted Spenz, drawing back the plush heavy velvet curtain.

"Achtung!" rapped Barnetschon, pushing Spenz to one side. "Ze blackout, dumkopf! You know ze rules!"

There was a knocking at the door. The men scuffled hurriedly back to their bunks.

"I say, can I come in?" came the genial voice of Commandant Betjeman.

"Herrein!" rapped Barnetschon, beads of perspiration breaking out on his forehead.

"Ze map!" hissed von Wankel.

It was too late. Buffy was already in the cell, beaming at the prisoners.

"Anyone like to come down and listen to my wireless set? Tommy Handley's on, it's jolly funny and Vera Lynn's on afterwards. She's smashing. D'you know 'We'll Meet Again'? It's awfully good, isn't it?"

Barnetschon gritted his teeth. It was more than he could bear.

"You still heff on your Zlippers, mein Kolonel!" he screamed with suppressed fury.

"So I have," lisped Buffy, absent-mindedly. "Silly old me! I say! Look at that lovely old Ordnance Survey map with 'Escape Route' written on it. What a pity it's been spoiled by someone scribbling over it!"

After he had left, von Wankel rushed to the map and quickly hid it under the floor-boards.

"Zis schweinhund Betjeman, he sees everyzink!" he snarled. "Ve must make extra effort for our escape planz. Zis place Neasditz is like ze Inferno von Goethe. Nobody escapes. Ze valls close in until every livink think is crushed beneath its evil power!"

He threw himself on his bunk, his whole body taut with frustration and fury.

Spring had come to Neasditz. Crocuses bloomed in the small patch of earth outside Commandant 'Buffy' Betjeman's office on the ground floor.

But the coming of the warmer weather only served to heighten the pent-up frustration of the three top-ranking German prisoners in D Block. Spring for them merely served to mark the beginning of yet another year of life in the most ruthlessly efficient POW camp in the whole of the British Isles.

"So! Ve heff five minutes before zat schweinerei Florrie Nabarro brings us ze afternoon tea und kek," snapped Barnetschon. "Is everyzink ready?"

The three men, Barnetschon, von Wankel and Spenz, for the last time checked their forged papers and equipment before setting out on one of the most breathtakingly daring escape attempts ever devised.

"Once more, plis, Spenz," von Wankel rapped. "If you are stopped, tell me who you are!"

Von Wankel drew himself up to attention: "I am Nigel Ponsonby Vodehouse," he recited. "I am travellink from my home von Virginia Vater to see mein Aunt in Princes Risborough, old boy, cholly good cricket, vat?"

"So, and vat are you doing in Neasden, my dear fellow?"

"I am prisoner of war!"

"Dumkopf!" yelled Barnetschon, his face empurpled with rage. "Ze answer is 'I am missink ze bus and is lovely day for a ztroll'. You vill get us all hung yet, you fool!"

From below came the cheery voice of Florrie Nabarro singing "Who do you think you are kidding, Mr. Hitler?" as she happily hoovered the carpet in the corridor.

The three men walked tensely towards the main gate. All of them felt strange and uncomfortable in their striped trousers, neatly blancoed spats and highly polished bowler hats.

The main gate was open. The doorman 'Old Bill' Grundy lay slumped, as usual, over an empty whisky bottle in his cubby hole.

"Vatever heppenz, keep valkin!" hissed Spenz, as they passed the recumbent Grundy and strolled out into Finefare Road.

Von Wankel could hardly believe their luck. They were free! He wanted to shout 'Heil Hitler!' It took all his determination, built up over years of training at Heidelberg, to restrain himself.

"So far so gut," whispered Spenz, giving his umbrella a nonchalant twirl. "25 metres vest zere is a bus stop. Ve get ze Number 94 to Cricklewood. Und next stop—Berlin!"

Still, he did not like the curious glances thrown in their direction by the passers-by.

"Luvverly violets?" An old woman called from her roadside basket.

"Nein!" snapped von Wankel. "I mean—not today grandma zank you ever so much duckie!"

Beads of perspiration broke out on his brow as they quickened their pace. Then, suddenly, disaster struck. As they turned the corner into Tesco Road they were confronted by the last man on earth they wanted to see.

"I say! Fancy meeting you three!"

It was Commandant Betjeman.

"Out for a stroll? Isn't it a lovely day? Look at that old George V Memorial Hall over there! It's the work of dear old Isaiah Wapping. No one remembers him now. I say, you're looking jolly smart all of you."

The three men dropped their umbrellas, turned on their heels and ran back into the camp.

Florrie Nabarro.

In their cell, Florrie Nabarro was pouring out the tea.

"So there you are! Where have you been, you naughty boys? I was just saying to myself, if they don't come back soon I shall have to make a fresh pot and no mistake!"

"Himmel!" screamed von Wankel, pounding his fist against the wall.

They were back to Square One.

Excitement ran high at Neasditz. That morning the Commandant, Col. Betjeman, had told the three German P.O.W.'s, Spenz, von Wankel and Barnetschon, to expect a new arrival in their quarters.

Now they watched from their high window on the first floor as the quietly purring taxi drew up in front of the Commandant's office. Out of it stepped a tall, sprightly figure in immaculate uniform. Col. Betjeman shuffled forward and paid the taxi.

A few minutes later the Commandant was ushering the newcomer into the cell.

"Well! Here you are, old boy! These chaps will show you the ropes. There's two blankets on the bed and a hot-water bottle if you need it. Florrie comes in to do for us twice a week. If you want anything else–just let her know. By the way, breakfast is at half past nine, but there's no need to rush."

As he doddered out, the new prisoner clicked his heels and sprang to attention.

"Major Chapman Pinscher reportink! Gentlemen!"

The three others raised their arms.

"Heil Hitler!"

The formalities over, Barnetschon waved to the departing figure of the Commandant.

"You can see ze kind of man ve are contendink viz in zis hell hole!"

He pounded his fist on the table.

"Is he alvays like zis?" asked Pinscher incredulously. "Old vorn out zlippers und dressink gown in ze middle of ze daytime to meet a Cherman officer?"

His keen grey eyes studied the silent faces of his fellow prisoners. Each one seemed to tell him what he feared most: that they were resigned to the idea of spending the rest of the war in Neasditz.

Pinscher adjusted his monocle and took a cigar from the box that the Commandant had kindly provided gratis. The others watched him as he sat down on his bunk,

Major Chapman Pinscher

crossing his legs and rubbing a thumb thoughtfully over the highly polished surface of his boot.

"Chentlemen!" he said, at last. "You know vat is ze matter viz you? You are not fit!"

Spenz was quick to riposte.

"Zis is not ze time for personal attacks on ze Kapitan," he said, glancing at Barnetschon's protruding stomach. "It's quite true. Ve eat very well here. Ve cannot help it. Cream buns for tea every day, und roly puddink vor afters. I tell you, my good friend, you vill soon be lookink ze same!"

Pinscher smiled icily.

"Chentlemen, you misunderstand me", he soothed. "Zink for a minute! For exercise ve need ze P.T. horse!"

A light of comprehension dawned in von Wankel's steely blue eyes.

"Ja wohl!" he cried. "Ze vooden horse trick!"

"Ssh!" hissed Spenz. "Ze Neasditz valls heff ears!"

The four German officers in "Cell 3" were strangely silent. Only that morning they had heard the news that their request for a wooden P.T. 'Horse' had been turned down as a result of acute shortages.

Major Chapman Pinscher, whose brainchild the wooden horse had been, was especially downcast.

He stood now at the cell window pensively drawing on a Corona Corona and sipping a schooner of Buffy Betjeman's home-made geranium sherry.

"Gott in himmel!" he muttered, "Dis Betjeman vins every demmed trick!"

From the courtyard below came the sudden cry, familiar to generations of Englishmen, "How's that?"

The four men crowded round the window.

"Vat are zey doink?" enquired Pinscher, his tight Germanic features creasing in a puzzled frown.

Spenz adjusted his gold-rimmed monocle and peered down into the courtyard.

"Ach!" he rasped, turning away in disgust. "Dis damfool cricket de English are alvays playink in summer!"

"Hittink a ball around viz a stick like a lot of schulekinder!" added von Wankel with a snarl of contempt.

"Look!" cried Barnetschon, pointing to the figures below, "look at dis trunkenschweinhund Grundy hittink ze ball over ze wall and hevink to go and get it!"

They all laughed cruelly as the gatekeeper "Old Bill" Grundy went puffing out of the main gate to retrieve the lost ball.

All but Pinscher turned away and flopped down despondently on their bunks.

Only the Major remained looking out absorbing the scene below.

Suddenly he clicked his heels and snapped his fingers.

"Heil Hitler!" he cried, "Spenz, mein freund! Barnetschon! von Wankel! Kommen zie hier! Ve are all of us now ever so keen to learn zis vunderbar English cricket! I am now goink in person to see Betjeman and to acquire ze book of rules. Owzat, my friends?"

Obergruppenfuhrer Spenz.

Pinscher laughed sardonically and frog-marched from the room.

Barnetschon, looking at the empty glass of sherry, said with a sigh: "Vat did I tell him. A few veeks in zis hell hole is makink him crazy like all of us. Poor chap! Poor old Pinscher! He is crackink up pretty damned fast!"

"Hard in, Bill, old chap!"

Commandant Betjeman called from the wicket as von Wankel, his brilliantly blancoed pads flashing in the hot August sun, came scurrying into his crease.

It was the first time that the German prisoners of war had been given a taste of "ze damnfool Englisch cricket" as Spenz had called the game.

But these desperate men were not playing for fun. Behind their suddenly acquired enthusiasm for the game lay a brilliant master escape plan devised by Major Chapman Pinscher.

Von Wankel made his ground and snarled with impatience as he watched Old Bill Grundy at mid-wicket fumble with the ball and throw high over wicket keeper Betjeman's head making the Commandant jump in the air. His old grey flannels ripped with the strain and fell into a dishevelled heap around his legs.

"Phew!", he gasped, "I think it's about time for tea, don't you, old sport?"

"Vait till ze end of ze over, schweinhund!" von Wankel spat the words out in a fit of uncontrollable temper. Even when they were playing their own national game, all that the proud Panzer commander and brilliant strategist could see was bumbling inefficiency.

After tea the Germans declared at 379 for no wicket and it was now the turn of Betjeman's XI to face the pace bowling of Pinscher and Spenz.

Betjeman and Grundy, their ill-fitting pads and old sweaters contrasting strangely with the immaculately creased flannels of their opponents, shambled towards the wicket amidst polite applause.

The Commandant took guard and settled himself to await Pinscher's first ball. The tall German pounded down the pitch and released a delivery that shot past the Commandant's head like a mortar-shell.

Betjeman wiped his brow.

"I say, gosh!" he gasped. "Hang on a minute, major. Bill! Give me a hand with the sight screen will you?"

The Germans watched in motionless horror as the two British batsmen reached the great white screen and pulled it to one side.

There, standing in a hole already waist high, stood the perspiring figure of Barnetschon, shovel in hand.

"Mein Gott!" he snarled, "Fooled again!"

Excitement in the German quarters was at feverpitch. That night was to see the one and only performance of '*Just Who Are You Kiddink Herr Churchill?*', the revue put on by the prisoners to entertain their British captors.

But behind the fun and games lay a deadly serious and brilliantly conceived escape plan devised by Major Chapman Pinscher. This time there would be no mistakes.

As Barnetschon had said: "Zis plen is foolproof".

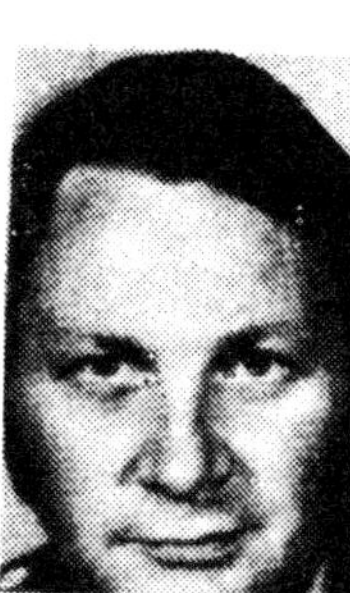

Promptly at 8 o'clock in the makeshift canteen theatre, the lights dimmed and von Wankel struck up the *Blue Danube* on the old camp piano.

Commandant Betjeman, the janitor "Old Bill" Grundy, and Florrie Nabarro settled themselves in the front row, as the curtain rose to reveal Barnetschon dressed in dressing gown and slippers over a British officer's uniform.

"Hello, old cheps", he started, "und welkommen to the show. Ahem!"

He waited, looking nervously into the wings.

"Ahem!"

"Cor e's gorn and forgotten 'is lines!"

Florrie Nabarro began to titter.

"Vat are you leffink at", screamed Barnetschon, his face purple with anger.

Commandant Betjeman clapped his hands with pleasure.

"Gosh! I say! This is jolly good fun, isn't it? Old Barnetschon dressed up to look like me. Look, who's this?"

Onto the stage stumbled Spenz, clean-shaven, with a broom in one hand and a bucket in the other. He wore an old flowered apron and had a cushion stuck under his jumper.

"Hello boys, vant a nice cup of tea dearies", he cried in a falsetto snarl, emptying the contents of his bucket over Barnetschon's head.

Betjeman doubled up with laughter. Tears streamed down his face as he clutched his sides. Old Bill Grundy snored contentedly beside him.

"Und now ze interval, sank you so much", said Pinscher from behind the curtain.

The lights came on and the Commandant lit his pipe. Half an hour later, the audience were still waiting for the entertainment to resume.

"Bloody long interval if you ask me, dearie", cried Florrie at last. "Come on, Fritzy, lets be 'avin' yer!"

But no sound could be heard from behind the scenes.

"I say d'you think they're alright back there?" asked Betjeman. "I'll just go and see what's holding them up."

He shuffled forward and peeped behind the curtain.

The stage was bare and of the German prisoners there was no sign—only a note pinned to the Dressing Room door: "Goodbye Buffy Old Bean".

Out in the cool night air, the four Germans, still wearing their costumes, strode confidently through the crowded streets of Neasden.

Everyone was dancing. Fireworks exploded in the sky. Churchbells rang out and old age pensioners joined hands with teenagers.

"We are free my friends!" shouted von Wankel above the noise. "Next stop Berlin and to a little place I know just off ze Luftwaffeplatz vere you can get pretty good apfelstrudel for only three pfennigs. Und you should see the frauleins, nichtvar!"

Suddenly Pinscher stopped dead in his tracks and pointed to the *News Chronicle* placard outside the Underground station.

"WAR IS OVER—OFFICIAL".

"Himmel!" he snarled. "Foiled again!"

THE END

My wife always wanted SECURITY..
well, she'll be secure enough in here...

secure enough

CEMENT

John Glashan

"All those in favour raise their right leg"

Monkey House "Out of control" claims keeper

by Our Zoo Correspondent
CONSTANTINE FITZBABOON

Britain's monkey houses are once again in a state of ferment. The astonishing scenes which we have witnessed in the past few days are reminiscent of the worst excesses of 1968.

Perhaps the supreme irony is that the worst outbreaks have occurred at a monkey house which the experts all agree gave the monkeys "the finest environment any monkey could ask for".

The open-air monkey house at Colchester, Essex, was specially designed by Col. Reuben Prefab RIBA to give the monkeys "a real chance to find a meaningful role".

ABOMINABLE SLOMAN

The Head Keeper, Dr. Fred Sloman, was personally selected as a man who had a unique sympathy with monkey aspirations.

And yet five years after the enclosure was personally opened by Her Majesty the Queen, the dream of a new liberated environment, where monkeys could engage in significant dialogue with their keepers, has become a squalid nightmare.

Today I saw the Essex monkey-house with my own eyes. Everywhere little groups of dirty, unkempt animals were lounging about the "campus". Much of the time they just sit, scratching at their long hair, and gazing vacantly into space.

Then suddenly one will stand up and utter incoherent grunts, such as 'Pigs Out'. The rest will then follow him, gibbering, and engaging in meaningless bouts of violence, such as hurling refuse at anyone who comes near them.

CLOCKWORK ORANG

This afternoon the Chief Keeper, Dr. Sloman, appeared to have given up any attempt to preserve the vestiges of discipline.

It is now nearly a week since Dr. Sloman barricaded himself in his Keeper's Shelter, and refused point-blank to emerge until the monkeys "came to their senses".

Dr. Sloman's action has only infuriated the monkeys even more. Last night they crowded around his shed, howling abuse and throwing ripe bananas through the already broken windows.

GORILLA WARFARE

But Assistant Keeper Prof. Vladimir Ilyich Tomkinson, 26, said "It is only a tiny minority of the monkeys who are responsible for these acts of violence.

"The vast majority want to get on with scratching, copulating and eating bananas, just as monkeys have always done. These monkeys are well-fed, well-housed and come from good jungles. They know they have no real cause for complaint."

Even so, the latest disorders at Colchester and Oxford have revived the cry that the monkey-houses should be drastically reformed, and cut in numbers.

There are at present in Britain 2,511 institutions with the full rank of monkey-house, and 621 polytechnics.

Dr. Rhodes Boyson is 112.

LETTERS TO THE EDITOR

From Sir Herbert Gussett

Dear Sir,

May I use your columns to express my wholehearted support for the firm stand which the Home Secretary Mr Roy Jenkins has taken in the face of what amounts to little more than blackmail. Recent kidnappings have brought home to us all the very real danger facing man, woman and child throughout the civilised world.

Who next? It is a question no-one can answer and few dare to ask. I venture to suggest that these extremists could even enter my own home and kidnap my lady wife whose name, as regular readers of my letters will tell you, frequently escapes me. Few women are so reckless of their own safety and would make themselves so easily a prey of these crazed terrorists.

Wednesday would be a good day. She goes to the shops on her bicycle leaving the house punctually at 9.30 and travelling northwards down Badger Lane. At Widdicombe Meadow she has to dismount and wheel her machine across the field. This would be an ideal moment for the kidnapper to strike. He might bundle her into a landrover and drive across country and within 20 minutes be speeding down the M4 to Bristol where a boat could ferry them both out East, where there are so many sights with which I have been familiar in days of yore.

Even at night my wife takes no precautions against personal attempts on her safety. Her bedroom is on the first floor with a window, habitually left open, second from the right as one looks at the house from the road. An intruder could use the ladder which is in the garage (door always open) and gain access to my wife's room with little difficulty. I should mention that I am a heavy sleeper and that it is highly unlikely that I would hear the loudest noises, whatever these might be.

I have said enough, I hope, to convey the very real danger which confronts my wife by day and night. I need only add that in the event of a successful kidnapping I am sure, according to my own lights, that I would emulate Mr Jenkinson in every respect and refuse to budge an inch. For, as Kipling says:

"Once you give Johnny Gyppo ten rupees You'll never get rid of the fellah, What ?"

I remain, Sir,
SIR RUDYARD GUSSETT
Dames Bottom
Bucks.

"If you're looking for evidence of corruption, Inspector, you'll be leaving empty-handed"

THE GREAT NARG WILL DRAMA

by ZANTINE COMPLEXITY

In the notaire's office next to the church in the tiny, sun-drenched Auvergne village of Mouzac, the opening shots were fired last week in a 10,000 million franc war of nerves that will make Vietnam look like a Sunday-school production of *Last Exit to Brooklyn*. The battle is on – to decide just which of Pablo Narg's 79 illegitimate great-grandchildren is to inherit the most valuable collection of money the world has ever known.

For over 100 years the genius of Pablo Narg towered over the whole world. During his life he had everything he wanted – lovely women, fast cars, sundrenched villas, After-Eight mints.

But today Pablo Narg has left behind him a legacy of hatred. For behind the battle over Narg's will, lies an intrigue of almost Byzantine complexity.

Perhaps the supreme irony is that, throughout his life, Narg was an untiring campaigner in the cause of world peace. And yet today, in the tiny, sundrenched Auvergne village of Mouzac, the opening shots are being fired in a 20,000 million franc war (contd. plage 94)

THE CLAIMANTS

NARG–the tormented genius whose 80-year career was one long battle against convention.

EDWIGE NARG–'La Mama'–Narg's first wife, who bore him 3 children and also bored him, which is why he left her in 1902. She died in 1921.

SIR ROLAND PENROSE, one of Narg's most devoted admirers. Though no relation, he says he would still like to 'get in on whatever's going'.

JUANITA STRETA-PORTA, orange-haired Cockney starlet who comforted Narg during his declining years.

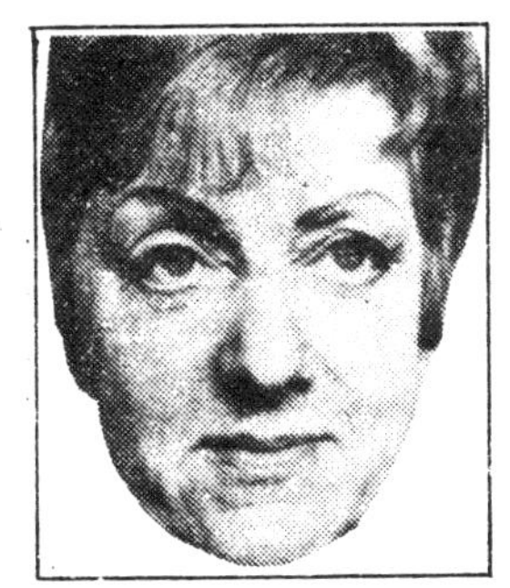

AMMONTILLADA CHEVROLET—'El Slagheap'—the passionate Catalonian beauty who lived with Narg in his Paris studio for three weeks in 1903. She died in 1936.

MANUEL DE MANHOLÉ— Barcelona street sweeper, who claims to be Narg's fifth-cousin twice-removed.

'EL CLARKO'—torrid, moody bull-fighter who posed for many of Narg's more controversial canvases. Shot in Spanish Civil War, 1937.

KEVIN PABLO PROUST, 8, Narg's great-great-grandson by his fifth wife, Flamenco dancer 'La Berensonia'.

Public Appointments — £20,000 plus

Very Important and Highly Paid Legal Post in Manchester

(shortly to be renamed PERSONCHESTER)

Applications are invited for the post of Chief Assistant Senior Legal Advisor to the Non-Discrimination Assessment Planning Commission Research Unit. The salary payable will be in the Civil Service (Senior Assistant Deputy Principal) range of £18,625 - £40,216 p.a. Non-contributory pension at age 50, plus full Discomfort and Boredom Allowance.

The successful applicant will be required to adjudicate in sexist discrimination situations (as defined in the Equal Opportunities Act 1975) and to carry out prosecutions in the High Court. She (or he) or he (or she) will be expected to carry out such duties as:

a) Reading through small ads in the Manchester Evening News to see if they mention 'Girl Friday' or 'Doorman'.

b) Reading through all books used in schools and public libraries to eliminate all reference to discriminatory sex-role situations. This will involve the structuring of certain conventional sexist material, e.g. Shakespeare, Jane Austen, Dickens etc.

c) The ushering in of a totally new era, as laid down by statute, in which all domestic jobs, nappy-washing etc. shall be performed only by house-persons (i.e. men).

Apply to:

The Chief Person, Equal Non-Discriminatory Opportunities Commission (NW Area), 1004 Personchester 724 BL799.

NEASDEN BOROUGH COUNCIL invites applications for the post of

SENIOR DEPUTY COMMUNITY ROLE-MANAGEMENT AND PARTICIPATION CO-ORDINATOR

The precise nature of the job to go with this title has yet to be evaluated in concrete terms. But the salary will be in the range £14,301 - £16,789, plus full non-contributory pension, Removals Allowance of up to £1800, London Weighting Allowance, Luncheon Vouchers and free travel on Community Mini-Bus Service.

NEASDEN BOROUGH COUNCIL invites applications for RESEARCHERS

The task will be to evaluate and define the duties of the Council's new Community Role-Management and Participation Co-Ordinator (Senior Deputy). This very important post, shortly to be created, will play an on-going role in the Council's Job Creation programme.

Applicants must be at least 18, should have beards and speak with boring voices.

Salary Scale (according to age and lack of experience): £4,819 - £7,624. Apply to Researcher Application Officer, Neasden B.C., Floor 26, Kleenex House, P.G. Tips Road, N.27.

NEASDEN BOROUGH COUNCIL invites applications for the post of

RESEARCHER APPLICATION OFFICER

The successful applicant for this post will have to read through a lot of letters from men with beards and boring voices, and decide which lucky ones are to be paid £6,000-plus p.a. for doing nothing.

Salary scale: £7,612 - £9,240 plus free house, Ford Cortina, 14 weeks holiday a year, and Neasden Tedium Weighting Allowance of £1,200 p.a.

"I now declare these swimming baths open"

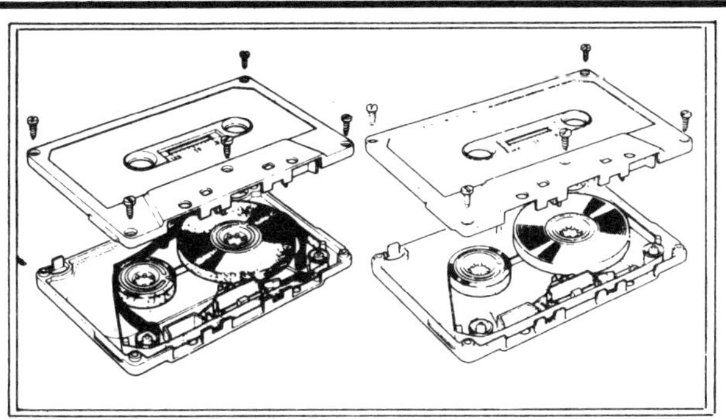

Rondello: Tapedeck (1973)

Contemporary Graphics

by

RAUSCH
de LUNI
SPIGGOTT
NODES
CARTER RUCK
BERGONZI
SCHIZOID
RONDELLO
EARACHE
WATSON
NUTTER
TUBULAR

KUNTZ

of Bond Street

Paris New York Zurich

BBC2

SECOND WIND

A Weekly Arts Magazine introduced by MELVYN BARG

BARG *(dressed in purple shirt)*: Hullo. Tonight in *Second Wind* we've got a new film on the potato-pickers of Cardiganshire, made specially for *Second Wind* by Doug Turd. Today is the birthday of the Newcastle folk-poet Geordie Broon – we've got a special anniversary tribute in song-and-mime compiled by the staff of the local community paper, *Tyne Out*. But first we take another look at a new type of music which is winning a great following across the Atlantic – Slim Longford's Appalachian Jug-and-Kazoo Footwarmers, one of the few surviving original Jug-and-Kazoo bands in the Appalachians. Here's Marty Milhench:

MILHENCH *(wearing purple check shirt)*: Slim Longford epitomises for me the whole essence, basically, of the Appalachian Sound. Slim has been connected with Appalachian music for over 70 years, but I am sure you will agree, his is a truly original voice. This film was made at last year's Ince-by-Makerfield Jug-and-Kazoo Festival by the Dutch film-maker Carlos Van Der Jogernaut.

FILM OF ANCIENT HILL-BILLY, VAGUELY RESEMBLING CLAUD COCKBURN, IN TARTAN SHIRT AND DRINKING FROM LARGE JUG.

SLIM LONGFORD *(sings)*:
Weall, ah gits up in de moanin . . .
Feelin' kind-a-blue

VIOLIN: *Whine, whine.*

GUITAR: *Plunk, plunk.*

JUG-AND-KAZOO: *Gurgle, gurgle.*

LONGFORD: *And ah justa kinda*
keep on thinkin'
of YEW!

VIOLIN: *Screech, screech.*

GUITAR: *Plunk, plink.*

JUG-AND-KAZOO: *Gurgle, hic.*

SHOT OF MAN IN AUDIENCE RESEMBLING DAVE SPART (for it is he) MOUTHING WORDS AND PICKING NOSE.

LONGFORD: *Ain't no danged good use a worryin',*
'Cos my Mary-Lou ain't there
etc. etc.

BARG: That was the authentic voice of Slim Longford, and the exciting camera work was by Clive Irving. *(COUGHS, CONSULTS NOTES).* Little magazines can have no circulation, and yet can continue to come out month after month, particularly if they have an enormous grant from the Arts Council. You've only got to think of the influence on the whole field of British literature of magazines like *Scratch*, *Poor Old Cow*, *Flux* and *Exchange and Mart* – all of them now recognised as seminal turning points, which gave us such new voices as George Boring, Abraham Watkins and Sylvia Flute. But this week sees something very special in British poetry magazine publishing. Here's a film made for *Bored Stiff* by A. Elvinoz.

SHOT OF PIN-UPS OUTSIDE SOHO STRIP CLUB. CAMERA PANS TO SHOW NONDESCRIPT YOUNG MAN WALKING GRITTILY DOWN GREEK STREET.

A. ELVINOZ: In recent years, many of us have come to recognise Ian Narg as one of the truly authentic and original voices in poetry. It is impossible to write a poem in Britain today without first measuring it against the coolly astringent criteria laid down by Narg from his Soho headquarters. And now, at the age of only 38, Narg takes a commanding step forward. With the full backing of the Arts Council, and the David Frost Foundation, Narg launches a new magazine – called *The New Magazine*.

GERTRUDE STEINER (SEEN RELAXING IN CAMBRIDGE GARDEN AT TAXPAYER'S EXPENSE): Well, I think zis is a most exciting day viz Narg's new paper hitting ze book-stands. Firstly it has contribution from me, and zecondly I see it has also contribution from you. So it must be good, nein? Also from Melvyn Barg, so it vill get good plug on ze TV, nicht war? But I have just ein leetl criticism. Vy must it be £25 a copy? Ve vish our vise vords to go into every home in ze land, no?

ELVINOZ: I can't agree with you there, Gert. It seems to me that there are only about three people left in this country who are intelligent enough to understand what we are trying to say–namely ourselves.

CUT TO NARG DISCUSSING PROOFS WITH BEARDED LAYOUT MAN.

VOICE OVER: Narg is obsessed by detail, and will often spend a whole day correcting one line. His taste is impeccable. Nothing is good enough for him. A word from Narg can make or break the reputation of a poet. Two years ago, after a damning review from Narg, the Australian poetess Daphne Balon threw herself off Tower Bridge. At the same time, Narg has made Elkan Foggis a household word.

FOGGIS *(wearing purple Kaftan and dark glasses)* RECITES IN FLAT NEW ENGLAND MONOTONE:

Black seagulls of the mind
Wheel and drone interminably
Down the freeways of
My life's voyage.
Hullo! Just a thought! Now Auden is
Dead, and
Also Pound Eliot Stravinsky etc.
Gone gone to the white walls
Of death.
Soon it will be me.

(SINGS)

Still, t'ain't a no good a worryin'
'Cos my Mary-Lou ain't there.

VIOLINS WHINE, JUGS-AND-KAZOOS GURGLE. ENTER SLIM LONGFORD, MELVYN BARG, IAN NARG, Dr. JONATHAN MAHLER, UNCLE KEN RUSSELL AND ALL. SHOWER OF ARTS COUNCIL CHEQUES POURS FROM CEILING ON ALL CONCERNED.

FADE.

Arthur Koestler's BELIEVE IT OR NOT

THE MYSTERIOUS ROOTS OF MEANINGFUL SYNCHRONICITY

Since I appealed last week for readers to send me their best "coincidence" stories, my post-bag has been fairly bulging, I can tell you! (*writes world-famous Viennese sage Arthur Koestler*).

Here is just one typical story, from *Sunday Times* reader E. Tharg of Nuneaton, Staffs.

Dear Old Codgers,

Some years ago I bought a budgerigar in a pet-shop in Bootle. My wife christened him Vercingetorix, after our goldfish who had just died. Imagine my surprise when the following Tuesday I noticed in the paper that the winner of the 3.30 at Kempton Park had also been called Vercingetorix.

Yours faithfully,
E. THARG

P.S. If you require independent confirmation, you can go to the British Museum, where I gather they keep all the newspapers going back to heaven knows when!

Equally extraordinary is the experience of Mrs. Doris Norris of Heckmondwyke:

Dear Arthur,

When I saw your your little competition for the 'funniest coincidence', I couldn't help being reminded of my Uncle Jim. On 3 April 1917, Jim was in the trenches in France when he was suddenly stung on the nose by a bee.

Forty years later to the day, on 3 April 1957, he was run over by a bus. It was a 17B!

Yours faithfully,
HORACE MORRIS (Mrs)
The Hive,
St. Bees, Cumberland

Here again we see clearly at work the mysterious force of what Jung has termed "coincidence". Mr. Morris could easily have been stung by a wasp, in which case the story would have been robbed of its almost eerie significance!

How can we explain such a mysterious phenomenon as this?:

Dear Professor Branestawm,

Last Tuesday evening I was watching TV, when weatherman Bert Ford came on and predicted that heavy rain would fall in all areas during the next 24 hours. Scarcely had he finished speaking, when I heard a strange sound from the garden outside. Imagine my surprise when, looking out of the window, I saw the first drops of a heavy shower beginning to fall! Incidentally my name is not exactly inappropriate!

Yours faithfully,
MONTY SHOWER
Waterford, Eire

Certainly rational science has no explanation for this kind of experience. History too is full of inexplicable coincidences. Take, for instance, this one, sent in by a Penge reader, Mr. Bernard Levin:

Dear Sir,

In 1912 the President of the United States was called Wilson.

In 1974, exactly 62 years later, the Prime Minister of this country is also called Wilson. President Wilson's Christian name was Woodrow, a very unusual name I am sure you will agree! Yet we also have a politician in this country called Woodrow—i.e. Woodrow Wyatt, formerly a member of Mr. Wilson's party. But the chain of coincidence doesn't stop there! One of the companies recently mentioned in connection with the Poulson affair was Taylor Woodrow. The historian A.J.P. Taylor has frequently written about Woodrow Wilson. Wyatt Earp, like President Wilson an American, was mixed up with Jesse James, the well-known outlaw. And James is of course the first name of Mr. Harold Wilson's colleague, Mr. Callaghan. To cap it all, Mr. Callaghan, like Mr. Wilson, Mr. Wyatt, Taylor Woodrow and Professor Taylor, has strong links with the Labour Party. If you wrote all that in a book no one would believe it!

Yours faithfully,
RALPH NUTTER
Maudling, Herts

But undoubtedly the coincidence story which wins this week's prize of a Dame Harold Evans Monogrammed Executive Backgammon Board—worth £15—comes from 5-year-old Keith Mitterand of Lime Grove:

Dear Uncle Arthur,

Last Sunday our family was all sitting round reading different parts of the Sunday Times *when suddenly we all shouted out at once, "Blimey, what a load of old rubbish!"*

Yours faithfully,
ENOCH NARG (49)
Fenton Villas,
Dempster, Staffs

"I now pronounce you man and. . . WAIT FOR IT!"

The Family

CONTINUING THE INTIMATE SERIES OF AN EVERYDAY FAMILY, LIVING NEAR SLOUGH.

Anne and Mark have moved away to live on their own.

SHOT OF ANNE IN HOUSECOAT HOLDING VACUUM-CLEANER STARING OUT OF WINDOW.

MARK: I'm off now then.
ANNE: Orlright

(LONG PAUSE)

MARK: Wassup with you then?
ANNE: Nuffink.

(VERY LONG PAUSE)

MARK: Well I'm off then. See you later.
ANNE: Ta ta.

GOES TO RADIO SWITCHES ON JIMMY YOUNG SHOW. STARES OUT OF WINDOW

JIMMY YOUNG: Hi there housewives. Here's a recipe for Roly Poly pudding.

FADE

THE QUEEN: Ere! Look at this then!
DUKE OF EDINBURGH (for it is he): Wossat?
THE QUEEN: Look wot this MP is sayink about us?
DUKE (Grabs paper): Oh it's 'im!

QUEEN MOTHER: Oo's that? Wossit say?

THE QUEEN: 'Sthat Willie 'Amilton again. You know that bloke what's always going on about us sayink rude fings an 'that.
QUEEN MOTHER: Bleedin' sauce! Oose 'e fink 'e 'is? I mean wots 'e know about it?

FADE

SHOT OF PRINCESS ANNE STILL STARING OUT OF THE WINDOW. THE ARCHERS ON RADIO.

INTERVIEWER: Are you finding it lonely living here?

(LONG PAUSE)

ANNE: 'Snot the same like it was at home.

FADE

THE QUEEN: What's up with you then?
CHARLES: Nuffink.
THE QUEEN: Sitting around the 'ouse all day.
CHARLES: Shurrup.
THE QUEEN: Nice talk that is. You don't use language like that when your father's 'ere.
CHARLES: Shurrup mum. I'm goin' out if you're goin' to keep on naggin'.
THE QUEEN: 'Bout time you got a job and settled down at your age.
CHARLES: Shurrup

FADE

World Cup

EL THARGO

Pin—Up of the Pampas

A Personality Profile by Private Eye's World Cup Reporting Squad

World Cup fever has certainly gripped all four inhabitants of the tiny, sun-parched Andean village of Santa Telegrafia—for this is the birthplace of the fabulous El Thargo.

Born fifteen years ago in a tiny lama herd's hut as plain Pablo Manuel Theotocoupolos de los Thargos, the Paraguayan striker today earns more than 25,000 million *bolivars* a year. He owns a string of boutiques, an airline and a ranch the size of Texas.

What is he like, the man on whom the 10 million soccer-crazy Paraguayans rest their hopes of bringing home the legendary Sir A.L. Rouse Trophy to sun-bleached *Asuncion*?

One thing is certain. The dusky senoritas of his native pampas certainly go wild over the husky heart-throb of the High Sierras they call "El Thargo".

M'THARGI

the cuddlesome Congolese

The war drums will certainly be beating tonight in the monsoon forests of Zsa-Zsa Gabon—for this is the birthplace of the legendary M'Thargi.

Born sixteen years ago in a little mud hut on the banks of the great Omo river, the 7'6" gentle giant from Gabon today owns a set of bongo drums, a shrunken human head and a loin cloth.

What is he like, the man the Scottish team have most to fear when they clash with Gabon in their vital Group Four encounter next week? One thing is certain. We know nothing about M'Thargi, since this is the first time he has ever seen a football in his life.

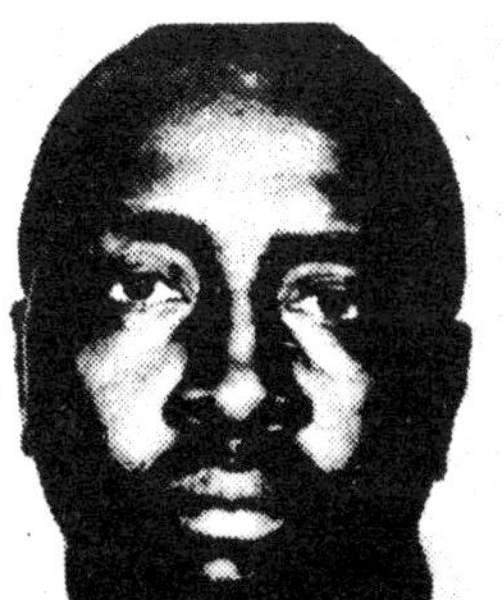

Haiti H-Bomb rocks Latvians

-many dead

Haiti 1 : Latvia 0

by PHEW WHATAMACILLVANEY

In the immortal words of W.G. Yeats, "things fall apart, the centre cannot hold . . ." and never was this truer than during the ninety-nerve-wrenching minutes in the sun-drenched Albert Speer Memorial Stadium here in Frankfurt this afternoon, where the moment of truth finally dawned for Senor Luigi Amontillado's eleven heart-broken Haitians as they bit the dust to the terrifying tornado that was the boot-to-ball blitzkrieg of the fearsome footballing fuehrers from the Finland Sea **(continued P.94)**

Security Screen Biggest Ever

Claims W. Germans.

"The biggest security operation ever mounted". That was the proud claim by Munich police chief Obersturmfuehrer Adolf von Pumperknacker yesterday, as he inspected some of the 4000 concrete artillery emplacements which have been set up as a first-line defence against Scottish fans.

"Ve are ready for anything" said a tired but triumphant Pumperknacker "nuclear attacks on ze stadiums, airborne assault by supporters von Tottenheim disguised as nuns—even your own Dad's Army has nossing on zis."

Obersturmfuehrer Pumperknacker is 53.

E.I. Addio Says: Two totally different philosophies of football clash next Thursday when Interflora's £2000 million striker Dina Zoff, playing for Bulgaria, meets canny defender Cornelius Berkhouwer, the dour Dutchman from Sanilav Yokohama. For Zoff football is a frenzied farrago of foul language and fisticuffs. For Berkhouwer it is more like a game of three-dimensional chess, with every move coolly planned years ahead by a brains trust of finely-honed computers.

ON OTHER PAGES

Results in Full . . . . . pp 8
"I Say If England Were Still In, They'd Walk Away With It"—Sir Alf . p 29
Wislon Flies to Munich—Picture . . . . p 30

"This might be a little painful, Mr. Gumshaw"

"Oh yes, we can change your spots. It's quite an operation, but we can do it"

It's been PREYING on my mind for some weeks now, that you might be enjoying yourself ...

MOTHS OF THE WORLD

John Glashan

"All my books are best sellers, but this unfortunately doesn't prevent me from being a very boring person to meet."

Radio3

JOHN CROMBY (counter tenor) is the soloist in this afternoon's production of Astori's Los Boros by the Hampstead Norreys Amateur Operatic Society.

8.00 News and Weather

8.05 Oosterhuis: Concerto for Hautbois and Strings. EUGENE SWANAGE and the Rochester Festival Orchestra.
Weiskopf: Piano Concerto No.105. SERGEI M'BOTO (Piano) & the Ugandan Philharmonic Orchestra conducted by Sir Idi Amin.
Niklaus: Sinfonia Concertante for five Trumpets and Harp. Orchestre des Trompettes de Paris. Conductor Humphrey Limoges.

9.00 News and Weather

9.05 This Week's Composers
Balogh & Kaldor
Balogh: Five Hungarian Folk-Songs (1932). Josef Kagan (Baritone). Marcia Williams (Piano).
Kaldor: Symphonic Poem: Ma Vat Ruislip Chamber Orchestra Conducted by Sir Leopold Git.

10.00 From the Hounslow Festival.
Organ Recital from the Church of St. Chad's, Redditch.
Beckenbauer: Toccata in D.
Nargs: Preludium (1961). WILFRED NARGS (Organ).

Let's have a TRIAL SEPARATION ... for about thirty-five years...

John Glashan

POETRY CORNER

FRIENDS OF THE EARTH

So. Friends
of the Earth.

Who are they?
No one seems
To Know.

And yet you
Read about them
Every day in
The newspaper.

I should like,
To think of
Myself as
A Friend of
The Earth.

But is it something
for Keith's mum?
I wonder.

E. Jarvis Thribb.

Medical Forum

Are beards dangerous?

by 'A DOCTOR'

More and more men are growing beards today and I am often asked in my capacity as a doctor whether there is anything damaging to the health about a beard,

Well, the simple answer is no. A beard, or *barbus barbus* as we doctors call it, is, or should be, if it is properly cared for, a completely safe appendage to the face or chin.

But, as with everything else there could well be occasions, albeit rare, when a beard may come to constitute a health hazard. In such cases a simple remedy might be to shave the beard off. But this is a drastic course of action, and before doing so you would be well advised to seek medical advice.

THE WIT AND WISDOM OF

EVELYN WARGH

(As Sold to David Astor)

Evelyn Wargh was without doubt the most colourful, rumbustious, controversial, eccentric, amazing, very wonderful figure of our times.

Now, for the first time, his close friend Christopher Nogreat-Shaykes has told the full, no-holds-barred story of Wargh's tempestuous career. The following are just some of the highlights of Shaykes' incredible narrative.

■ In the winter of 1947, Evelyn caught a fearsome cold. He was always an impatient invalid, and when his wife telephoned the local GP and asked him to call, we all feared for the consequences. Sure enough, no sooner had Dr Wells rung the door-bell, than Wargh seized a shot-gun and rushed to the porch. 'Pray state your business!' he shouted. Before the unfortunate medical man had time to reply, Wargh discharged a volley of shot over his head. As poor Dr Wells fled down the drive, I remarked to Evelyn that this was scarcely a very Christian way to receive a visitor. 'If I was not a Catholic,' he replied, 'I would have killed him.'

■ Lady Lavinia Strames has told me of the unhappy occasion when she once invited Evelyn to dinner, to meet some American friends. One of these happened to remark to him, 'My, Mr Wargh, I really enjoyed your latest book.' 'So did I, you silly little fool,' he replied. 'That's why I wrote it.'

■ After the war, during the period of shortages, one found it difficult to obtain a decent pair of shoes, and one was occasionally forced to somewhat unconventional resorts. I remember one day entering White's in a pair of bright green galoshes. Sitting in his usual position on the mantlepiece, was Evelyn. 'Where did you get those overshoes?' he shouted, his face contorted with rage and jealousy. 'Give them to me at once.' I refused, saying that I was particularly attached to the galoshes, which I had bought from Millett's for a duck-shooting party in Norfolk in 1925. Evelyn stormed out, but a few hours later he returned to the club in a pair of brilliant yellow spats, which he continued to wear until the time of his death, long after they had gone out of fashion.

A PRIVATE EYE CONDENSED BOOK

UP WITH THE CLARK

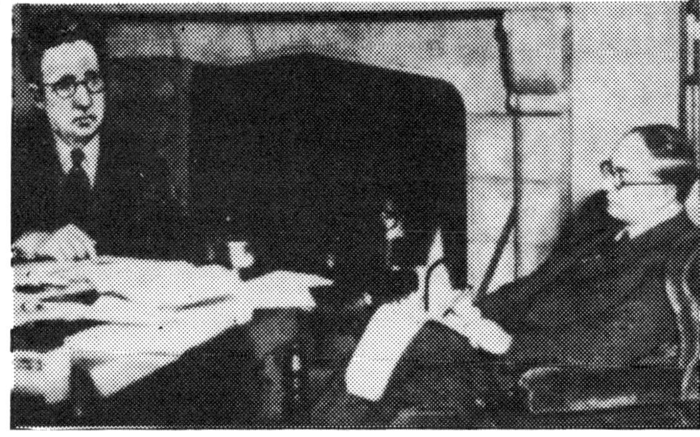

Lord Clark (*right*) with Bernard Bernardson

The Memoirs of Lord Clark of Civilisation

Many people have wondered why Lord Clark's autobiography has not been serialised in the Sunday Times. The reason is that the author has particularly requested that extracts should be published exclusively in what he himself describes as "Lord Gnome's agreeable little organ".

Chapter One: The Early Years.

I first realised where my true interests lay in life, when my father one day brought home from London a hideous nude by one of the most celebrated RAs of the day, Sir Archibald Narg. The painting, sixteen feet high, was placed in the billiard room at Crouchers, where my parents then lived. Upon seeing it for the first time, I remember bursting into tears — whereupon my father gave orders to Evans the butler to take it away and burn it. Although I was only three at the time, I realised at once that the only thing I wanted to do when I grew up was to help Mr Berenson rewrite his wonderful *Selezione di Pitturi Molto Agreable di Trecento di Calabria.*

Alas I could never feel enthusiasm for the normal pastimes of childhood, with the one exception of the game of marbles. Even to my insensitive eyes, these exquisite little balls of glass, with their wonderful interior *spiralismo* in all the colours of the spectrum, were a ravishing *coup d'oeuil.* I would contemplate them for hours in ecstasy. But soon, I am glad to say, childhood was over, and I went up to Oxford.

Chapter Two: I Meet All Sorts of Famous People

Undoubtedly one of the strongest influences in my life was my forty-year-long friendship with that remarkable man, Maurice Borer. Not only was he perhaps the greatest scholar of his time (he was perhaps the first person ever to appreciate the exquisite sweetness of the lyric poetry of Gladus Wislonius), he was also of course a tremendous wit. Alas, few of his jokes survive.

Other people I met at this time included Lady Utterly Immorell, T.S. Eliot, Cyril Connolly, John Betjeman, Arthur Negus, George V, Sir Roderick Glossop (later to be immortalised by P.G. Wodehouse) and John Wells. I also met Peter Quennell, who told me that I was "a stuck-up little aesthetic prig". Perhaps, who knows, he was right. But many people have since written to me saying how much they enjoyed my long-running television serial *Civilisation Street.*

Chapter Three: Italian Siesta

Then followed one of the most agreeable periods of my life. I went to Italy and, for the first time, came face to face with many of the masterpieces which I was later to make famous — Tomaso Driberghi's ravishing *Assumption*, the Lamborghini tryptych, the cloisters at Trattoria di San Alvaro, and of course the irresistible Bari Fantoni. I was also given an introduction to the greatest *connoisseur* of our time, Bernardo Levini. A small, dapper figure, with a great love of women and exquisite hands, he at once invited me to assist him in an unpaid capacity with the preparation of a new exhibition at his now legendary cartoon gallery in Gloucester Road. It was thus that I became acquainted with the work of such fine artists as Jak and Sprod, many of whose originals hang on the walls of my new prefab in the grounds of Saltwood Castle to this day.

Chapter Four: I Meet More Famous People

Many people expressed surprise when I was appointed Director of the National Gallery, thinking perhaps that, at the age of 21, I was rather young for the post. Nevertheless it enabled me to meet many famous people, including the Queen Mother, Dame Myra Hess, Noel Coward, Winston Churchill, George VI and John Piper, and I venture to suggest that my tenure of office was entirely successful.

Despite all our glittering friends, however, I have never been happier than when in the company of real artists. Jane and I will always treasure the memory of the glorious evening we once spent in Hugo Prayermat's rather *degoutant* little bed-sitter in Putney. There was a distinct *nuance* of old cabbage leaves on the air which Jane and I found wholly *sympathique* as we ate baked beans out of the tin, and admired Hugo's agreeable collection of old socks.

All my life I have been a convinced Socialist, ever since I first came across a copy of *Das Kapital* in the library at Droppings. It was an exquisitely-printed edition by the Touchstone Press, with haunting illustrations by Arthur Rackham, and delicately pencilled marginalia by Paul Foot, the son of Lord Caradon. It was only then that I first became truly aware that there were other people in the world besides myself.

NEXT WEEK: The War Clouds Loom — Jane and I have tea with Neville Chamberlain.

SAY GOODBYE TO PAINFUL CONSTIPATION

Three in every ten adults suffer from chronic constipation.

Often they are middle-aged men working in sedentary situations —lawyers, businessmen, etc.—the kind of men who can ill afford to spend valuable time waiting anxiously for nature to take its course.

Now at last Sutherland's, Makers of Laxatives since George the Third's Day, have produced the suppository that can eliminate those hours of painful expectancy.

SUTHERLAND'S SUPPOSITORIES

'Afore ye go'

On Sale At All Chemists

1. MARVO

2. MARVO

3. MARVO

4. MARVO

McLACHLAN

SUNDAY TIMES

weekly review

CLIVE JERK'S MEDIA TRIUMPH

On 5 May 1975, before a select but glittering audience in the foyer of the National Film Theatre, the distinguished litterateur Clive Jerk read out his new poem, A Farkin Load of Old Rubbish. *As Jerk intoned line after line of exquisitely-honed satirical verse, a frisson of ecstatic recognition rippled through the roomful of celebrities. Those present were at once aware that they had been privileged to witness the genesis of a masterpiece, one which, according to Ian Narg, editor of the prestigious* New Pseud's Monthly *(Back Numbers still available at £25 each), "must rank with Byron's Don Juan, the Satyricon of Petronius and the Vanity of Human Fishes". Today Jerk's masterwork, illustrated by Merc, is published in a Very Wonderful and Highly Desirable Limited Edition of only 200,000 copies.* Private Eye *is honoured and privileged to bring you Jerk's 20th century classic at a fraction of its normal price.*

Clive Jerk first came to England from Australia,
Determined at all costs not to be a failure.
To Milton's alma mater in the fens he trod,
And settled down in *Trinity Great Quad.*
But soon he tired of Academe's ways
And to the media turned ambitious gaze.
(For all the joys of cloistered scholasticity
You miss out on the money and publicity.)
And so he sold his talents to *Granada*,
To play the part of the poor man's Noel Picarda.
On 'Cinema' he puffed the current movies
To hosts of cineastic groovies.
From there his net spread far and wide,
His by-line soon all over was espied.
From Dylan-style lyrics to the *TLS*,
Jerk surely showed no *slothfulness.*
Pop concerts he reviewed in periods sesquipedelian
And *Proust* in jive talk, just to prove he could be a hip literary chameleon.
For years Jerk toiled, with unremitting fervour
Reviewing *Upstairs Downstairs* for the *Observer.*
But still the obstinate spark of fame remained unlit,
Till finally on this fantastic idea he hit;
i.e., using the pseudonym "CLIVE JAMES",
To write a poem dropping hundreds of famous names.
By putting them together in this sort of sub-heroic metre,
He could soon have a slim volume that would be a world beater.
And as for the right names to vilify,
He had only to turn to that week's *Private Eye.*
Dr Jonathan, the Blessed Arnold, Lady Magnesia;
Could at a flick of the pen be translated into 'Dr Fringe', 'Lord Fatman' and 'FREESIA'.
Within three days the mighty Ode was writ,

Neither *Juvenal* nor *Pope* would have been ashamed of it!
Of all the most famous media folk, not one was forgotten,
From *Lord Clark of Civilisation* to *Billy Cotton.*
The manuscript was sold for ready cash
To that frightful little creep at Cape's. Tom Mash.
But for Jerk much greater honour lay in store,
As news of his masterpiece penetrated to the *Sunday Times*'s Sixth Floor.
"This boy's a genius!" cried the Lilliputian DAME,
"The world can never be again the same.
"Stop the presses, hold the *Bruce Page*,
"This poem's the marvel of the age.
"For stuff like this, I'll pay ten grand.
"It's the first poem I've read I can understand.
"You can get through the lot in half a minute,
"Besides, I've heard of all the people in it."
And so, with a cry of "Life's a challenge, like,"
He headed for Bloomsbury on his motor-bike.

For a week or more, Jerk's fame was astronomical —
"*Brilliant*", "*Amazing*", "*Exquisitely Comical*",
"*JERK IS THE KING — Don't be deluded*"
The critics cried (all having been included).
And so, for our hero, the streets ran with milk and money
(What no-one pointed out was that his poem was not particularly funny).
The other point of course was that if the poet had really done his work,
The first name in his gallery of media pseuds and bores should have been *JERK.*
(or words to that effect.)

An Exhibition of the Original Fine Artwork illustrating "Clive Jerk's Media Triumph" by Merc is currently on show at Crooks and Pooves Very Wonderful Old Paintings Ltd., Bond Street.

"A slice of bread has enough nutritional value to feed a family of 4 for three weeks."

So says Dr. R. B. D. Kohnmann Professor of Diatetric Studies at Breading University and author of the best-selling book "Who's Who in the Bread World."

Fact

Dr. Kohnmann knows more about bread than any other living individual.

Today's loaf is bigger, more health-giving and protein-packed than ever before (see *The Nutritional Structure of Bread Particles: An Analysis* by Prof. J. Crumbs and Dr. Stephen Toast M.D.). Why?

Lots of reasons. To begin with the modern housewife looks for more in her bread than flour and water. She wants her loaf to be dietetically balanced, nutritionally beneficial and choc-a-bloc with hydromycin B, mydrohycin C, sodium maximum glotamin, E13 and everything that contributes to strong bones, bright eyes and an active married life.

See for yourself the comparative nutritional values of a random sample of everyday items:

YOUR GRAINS TONIGHT					
	%MG	Lab.	Lyco-Globulin	Road-holding ability	All Voters
28 oz White starched wrapped pre-stressed loaf (steam-baked)	99%	98½%	100%	99.98%	100%
Handful of beach sand (6 oz)	0%	0%	0%	0%	0%
Old Socks (slightly foxed)	0%	0.0001%	0%	0%	-0.01%
Fresh sawdust	0%	0%	0%	0%	0%
Daily Telegraph (standard size)	%	N.A.	%	0%	0%

No-one is saying that meat is dangerous. Even so there are plenty of scientists and doctors who warn us that some foods play an active role in causing chronic and sometimes fatal diseases.

Danger Code

	Mortality Rate
Bread	0%
Arsenic	100%

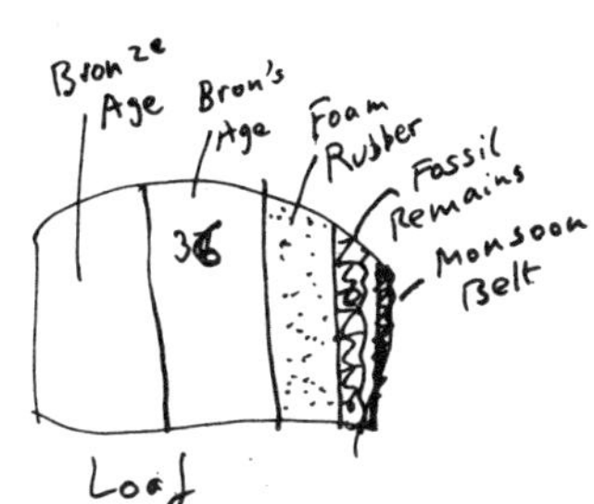

How the Government uses its loaf

It makes sense doesn't it? No wonder that your government has taken steps to see that everyone gets his fair share of the loaf.

A special committee maintains a round-the-clock watch on the British baking industry to ensure that the standards laid down in the 1947 Composition of Basic Baking Flour Act are adhered to in all respects.

You still hear people who are prepared to say "Bread isn't what it was". But Scientific Tests show beyond any doubt that bread baked in 1830 was markedly inferior to Today's Super Loaf.

Today's loaf is cheap and easily accessible. It comes ready cooked and hygienically wrapped. You don't even have to cut it. Buy some bread and find out for yourself the truth of Dr. Kohnmann's amazaing claim: "Two average-sized crumbs of bread contain more vitamins, minerals, proteins, carbo-hydrates, hormones, ameno-acids, molecules and honest-to-goodness energy than a plate of steak and kidney pie, ½ pound of potatoes, three hard boiled eggs, 3lb. grapefruit segments, 2 dumplings, 3 oz. halibut (lightly boiled), 4 roast oxen and eight tons of chips."

ISSUED BY CONGLOSSE ARS-LIKKER & TWYTTE (PUBLICITY) LTD. ON BEHALF OF THE BRITISH FLOUR ADVISORY COUNCIL FOR THE ADVANCEMENT OF THE CONSUMPTION OF GREATER QUANTITIES OF BREAD.

The Borer World

by Anthony Widmerpowell

In this exclusive extract from a forthcoming book, *The Zany World of Sir Maurice Borer,* one of the last remaining masters of the classical English prose style brings to life one of the greatest men of the 20th Century.

I first met Maurice Borer (I think) one afternoon – or was it a morning? – of the Hilary Term of 1925. I was living in digs in Hinksey with Giles (although in those days we all called him "Max", quite why I cannot recall) Brandreth, and that morning, or possibly it was the afternoon (one seldom saw him in the morning), Borer came round to borrow some sugar (or it may have been margarine, I cannot remember).

Although he said nothing which I can recall on that occasion, it was a memorable moment for me, since his reputation as the most brilliant wit among the younger dons of the time was at its height.

It was some months later before we were formally introduced, at a dinner party in Christ Church given by a mutual acquaintance Humphrey Lyttleton (one of the famous Eton Lyttletons, who in those days was a brilliant batsman, although he later became best known as the *grande eminence* of the National Theatre). A fellow-guest (clad I recall in brilliant maroon rugger socks, and speaking volubly about "la divine Rimbaud") was Enid Starkie, who monopolised the conversation to such effect that poor Borer said nothing throughout the evening, and left early saying that he had "some exam papers to mark". A typical Parthian shot!

Maurice at this time was one of the most generous hosts in Oxford, but it was very easy to get dropped from what he called his "list". If that happened, and it happened to almost everyone at one time or another, one was instantly categorised by Borer as "a bloody shit". The expression (possibly garnered from Thackeray's *Book of Shits,* of which Maurice, typically, had one of the only copies outside the Bodleian) conveys better than any words the fierce but generous-hearted way in which Borer looked upon his fellow men.

One story from this period which evokes the vintage Borer better than any is the celebrated affair of Lady Utterly Immorrell's *Sunday Telegraph*. Maurice was staying at Garsington on a week-end party, and came down to breakfast before any of his fellow-guests. He picked up the freshly-ironed copy of the *Sunday Telegraph* (or was it *The Observer*? – I cannot recall) and with characteristic vigour, proceeded to read it.

A few minutes later, Lady Utterly herself swept in, and (in that high-pitched nasal whine which was to be Britain's secret weapon in World War Two) announced to the company "Some bastard has swiped my *Sunday Telegraph*!"

Maurice was not in the least put out, and tearing the paper neatly into shreds, scattered them in the air. He was never invited to Garsington again.

Sometime in 1936, I succeeded in offending Maurice deeply, although just what the *casus belli* was I never knew. (It may have been my failure to comment on his new tweed suit, of which he was inordinately proud, because for the first time in his life, he said, he felt "well dressed" – a very important expression in the Borer circle, and a term of approbation merited by few. The rest of the world comprised "scruffy trogs", not to mention, of course, "bloody shits").

Whatever happened, Borer refused to speak to me for the next forty years. And then, suddenly, when I was staying with my grandfather down at Aldershot, he drove up in a Rolls-Royce with Lord Clark, insisting that the three of us should "go out on the piss for old times' sake." It was typical of Borer that, when the moment arose, he should be so quick to forget a quarrel.

Later in the evening we played darts, and Maurice won. "You've won" I remember saying to him. "No," he said sadly, "I've never won." But he had.

© Anthony Widmerpowell & Moggtrash Enterprises Ltd.

Radio

It's Your Line to George Gale

(Advert jingles fade away)

Gale: Hullo?
Man (*for it is he*): Hullo Mr Gale.
Gale: Yes?
Man: Er I've read in the newspapers I don't know if you've seen this about being able to claim back on sickness benefits when the party involved is registered self-employed.
Gale: I see. What about it?
Man: Well, is it right?
Gale: Is what right?
Man: Well, what I'm saying basically is I mean I'm only quoting from what I read in this morning's paper. Well as I said can I claim a zero-rated status on the two-tier system of VAT with self-employed benefits accruing?
Gale: I haven't the foggiest idea.
Man: Thank you very much Mr Gale.
Gale: Thank you Mr er er

(Contd Channel 94)

"How would you like your steak burned, sir?"

The Chalfont INTERVIEW with

His Imperial and Serene, Most Excellent and Puissant King of Kings and Only Ruler of Princes

THE SHIT OF PERSIA

(as seen on BBC TV)

(SHOT OF HUGE TRAFFIC JAM IN FRONT OF DISGUSTING CONCRETE OFFICE BLOCKS)

Chalfont: Iran is fast becoming the most powerful nation in the world. Tonight I am very privileged to be able to talk to the man who has made it all possible, His Imperial Magnificence, Adolf Narg.

(SHOT OF CHALFONT KNEELING IN ENORMOUS GILT ANTE-CHAMBER WITH HEAD BOWED AND TOUCHING SMALL BLACK SHINY OBJECT. CAMERA TRACKS AWAY TO SHOW SMALL BLACK SHINY OBJECT TO BE THE SHOE OF HIS VERY WONDERFUL AND HIGHLY IMPORTANT MAGNIFICENCE, KING TAMBURLAINE THE GREAT)

Chalfont: Your Serene Holiness, Iran is undoubtedly the richest and most advanced country in the world. How has this come about?

Shah: In my country the people work very hard. You in Europe do not know the meaning of work.

Chalfont: I do agree, Your Imperial Affluence. Though some people — only a tiny minority of course — people who have never had the honour of visiting your country — might suggest that some of your enormous wealth comes from the sale of oil. . . ?

(SHOT OF VAST PIPES AND DERRICKS STRETCHING TO HORIZON)

Narg (Reading from prepared script): The secret of my country's success is the state of complete trust that exists between me and my people. I trust them to do what they are told. And they trust me, because I have 1,000 tanks, 600 aeroplanes, and the most powerful army in the Middle East.

(SHOTS OF GOOSE-STEPPING SOLDIERS TRAMPLING OVER KURDS)

Chalfont: I would like to turn now to an extremely delicate question. . .

(WRINGS HANDS NERVOUSLY AND LICKS LIPS)

It has been suggested by, let me say at once, a very tiny minority of obviously misguided and probably left-wing people — people that is to say who are quite untrustworthy and know nothing about the very real problems that you face — these people, Your Holiness, have sometimes hinted that your government (and let me say at once that I dissociate myself entirely from such suggestions) has on occasion been forced to resort to somewhat coercive methods with regard to political prisoners. I need hardly say that you are entirely at liberty not to answer that question.

Ghengiz Khan: Oh good heavens, my dear fellow, of course we torture people. We're not living in the Middle Ages. We use the very latest techniques.

Chalfont (laughing with relief): Ha Ha. Quite so. I so agree. We too have our 'subversives'.

Shah: And you too torture them, no doubt?

Chalfont: Of course, of course. Well, thank you very much indeed Your King-Size Supreme Essence of Righteousness. I'm afraid that's all we've got time for this week, but I'm sure you'll agree that Iran seems a very wonderful and interesting place.

(CLOSING SHOT OF HUGE TRAFFIC JAMS, CONCRETE OFFICE BLOCKS, FLAMING OIL DERRICKS AND GOOSE-STEPPING SOLDIERS)

(A BBC-Time-Life Co-Production)

Medical Forum

How much money do we need?

By 'A Doctor'

Even though man has set foot on the moon there are some things we still know precious little about. Take money for example. How much do we need to sustain us in a normal living situation? Certainly some people appear to exist on hardly any, and to all intents and purposes manage to be cheerful enough. But take another example – we doctors. It now seems almost certain that doctors, unlike some other groups in the community situation, require a good deal more money if they are to give to the best of their ability. Scientific evidence has proved that a doctor may need four or five times more money than anyone else. Indeed, it is quite common for a doctor to have anything up to £15,000 per annum, and still feel the need for more. There's no harm in needing more money. It's a perfectly natural phenomenon. But if you feel that you have too much money, the best thing is to see a doctor and he will do his best to remove it.

After all, that's what we doctors are here for.

Two to share Gnome Prize

Telephone

Nevererdova

After the toughest battle in the long three-year history of the prestigious £10 Gnome Fiction Prize, it was announced that for the first time the award is to be shared between two of the three judges.

They are Mr Sid Telephone, author of *Grapefruit Segments,* and Miss Nadir Nevererdova, the Hungarian-born dental assistant whose first novel *The Last Tram From Newport Pagnell* has yet to find a publisher.

Announcing the awards at a celebrity-packed lunch at London's prestigious Old Jolyon's Golden Egg Take Away, was Lord Longford, father of several of the competitors.

In his congratulatory speech, Lord Longford said: "As a Christian and a publisher, I am always delighted to have the opportunity to talk about my new book, which is called *Jesus Christ Why Hasn't Anyone Bought It Yet?*

Pakenham In

Of Mr Telephone, the judges had this to say: "His name rings a bell".

They went on: "*Grapefruit Segments* is a masterly evocation of life behind the scenes in a British Rail Inter-City Dining Car. In delicate pastel shades of puce and orange, Mr Telephone paints a reticent canvas, rich in a suffused chiaroscuro of Brown Windsor soup and grapefruit chunks."

Miss Nevererdova was hailed by her fellow-judges as "an important new voice whose masterly evocation of life behind the scenes in the tram depot of a small Bedfordshire market town brings alive the whole rich canvas of everyday life in what has been called 'The Long Garden Party that was Edwardian England'.

"With wistful strokes," the judges continued, "Miss Nevererdova rips away the whole facade of hypocrisy that draped Edwardian piano legs, exposing the torrid, all-too-human passions which beat beneath the plus-fours and thick worsted socks of long-forgotten Bedfordshire artisans."

Melvyn Barg is 94.

A Book That Makes History.
Now at last available after 30 years
in preparation.

THE GNOME BOOK OF STONES

It's all here in this magnificent 5,000 page volume. The mysterious, the exciting world of stones.

Every day we tread on them, unaware of the fascinating facts that surround the apparently commonplace stone.

The author, Ephraim Peeble, formerly features editor of *Caravan Weekly*, says: "Until I began work on this book I knew nothing about stones. I came to them with an open mind. Soon I found myself caught up in one of nature's most extraordinary phenomena. My researches took me all over the world. I had studied literally millions of different stones before I sat down to write my book. I promise you that you will not be disappointed when you voyage with me into the extraordinary world of stones."

You will read of

The Amazing Leopard Stone of Paraguay

This stone is regarded by the local Ocuchu tribesmen as being sacred, with powers to heal or destroy.

The World's only edible stone from the foothills of the Himalayas

No bigger than a pinhead, this astonishing stone has been shown by scientists to contain minute traces of monosodium glutamate.

The Mighty Stone of Nargs

This giant boulder stands on a remote headland of the Isle of Sprod in the Outer Hebrides. It has long been thought by the islanders to mark the grave of Nargs, the legendary Celtic warrior.

Did you know?

There are no less than 10,000 different types of stone in one square foot of ground.

Just Think

TREASURE ON YOUR DRIVE

■ Ordinary looking gravel probably contains stones that were here aeons before the emergence of the pleiseosaurus.

Stones like the Litmos Neasdensis were once common. Why are they vanishing? Ephraim Peeble answers this question and many others.

HOW TO LOOK AFTER YOUR STONES

■ Stones are like anything else. They respond to care and attention. The **Gnome Book of Stones** illustrates with full-colour diagrams how to arrange your stones so as to obtain the maximum enjoyment from your collection.

★Over 800 pages of maps explain where you're likely to find stones.

Name that stone

400 page supplement shows easy method of how to identify any stone within a few seconds.

Offer applies U.K. only

This beautiful book, lavishly illustrated and bound in durable Scanlon, is something to cherish for the rest of your life. Available until 1989 at a SPECIAL SUBSCRIBER'S PRICE of £159.10 (+ p&p, VAT etc.).

SIGNATURE
(All orders must be signed by adult) . . . . . .

ADDRESS . . . .

. . . .

My card no. is 4 9 . 9

Dead should sue —says committee

by Our Legal Staff

Dead people in certain circumstances should be allowed to claim damages for libel, an official committee recommends today.

The Committee's Report, entitled 'Report of the Committee' (H.M.S.O. £5.70) says: "There has long been an anomaly in our legal system under which deceased persons are denied the right to issue writs, thus depriving many 'honest and hardworking lawyers' of the opportunity to earn even larger sums of money than they do at present."

Money

More and more people should be encouraged to sue, the committee says. At present many men and women are deterred by the prohibitive costs of litigation and the erratic behaviour of juries, thus depriving many 'honest and hardworking lawyers' of the opportunity to earn even larger sums of money than they do at present.

The members of the committee included: Mr Justice J.C.P. Throat-Pastille, Sir Julian Surtax QC, Mr Ephraim Sue (Senior Partner Sue, Grabbit & Runne), Mr Justice Nigger, Sir Humpty Cohen QC, an old man with a moustache whose name nobody knows, three other people and a woman.

Books

The strange death of Humphry Berkeley

by H. ROCHESTER POOVE
(Snipcock & Tweed £7.00)

Undoubtedly the funniest book of the year. Mr Poove has had the brilliantly witty idea of pretending to be an MP, using the marvellously pompous pseudonym, Humphry Berkeley MP. For the past ten years he has been writing a flood of absurdly facetious letters to all sorts of important people, including Mr Edward Heath, Sir Alec Douglas-Home, *The Times* and Mr Jeffrey Archer.

The extraordinary thing is that all these people appear to have taken him seriously – at least for a time. Many of them have even written back to him, and Mr "Berkeley" has had the brilliantly original idea of putting together their replies, and publishing them as a way of making a bit of money. The one I like best is the following deadpan answer from the Rt. Hon. Edward Heath:

Dear Mr Berkeley,

I am in receipt of yours of the 13th ult., and note the contents.

Yours faithfully,
RT. HON. E. HEATH,
Grocer Pursuivant to the Royal College of Harolds.

Psychology Today

About human experience · society and you

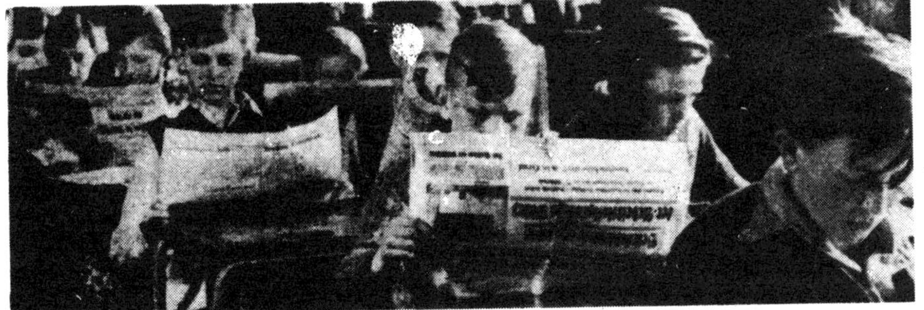

Seven out of every ten people would kill their fathers. Here's why they don't.

Psychology Today explains how we are all of us restrained from acts of violence only by an in-built response network.

Psychologists have discovered that even so-called 'normal' people are possessed by primeval instincts that go back to man's most primitive roots in the past, over 600 million years ago.

Other articles in this month's issue:

WHAT HAPPENS WHEN WE SNEEZE?

The latest scientific research proves that sneezing is a positive act of aggression. A handkerchief symbolically placed in front of the nose 'ritualises' the sneeze, thus defusing a potentially explosive situation.

TAKING THE DOG FOR A WALK

The instinct for power latent in every adult can be channelled into everyday activity situations. The dog provides a dual role both as the object of a male's natural desire to dominate and as a co-partner in his unconscious man=hunter role.

A DOUGHNUT IS A SEX SYMBOL

No one knows why people eat doughnuts. Even the name is a mystery. New evidence suggests that the doughnut is a highly charged erotic symbol and eaten only when the libido is challenged by some exterior threat.

WHY DO MEN SHAVE?

Shaving can be a sado-masochistic act. Three out of five men interviewed admitted to cutting themselves at least once a week. This is no accident, say psycho-analysts, but an aspect of 20th Century man's desire for catharsis in a guilt-situation.

NEW MAGAZINES

Leading Market Reserach men have proved, we hope, that normally sane men and women can be conned into paying 45p for a load of rubbish masquerading as bona fide research data clarifying our behaviour in a day-to-day situation.

At your newsagent's now. 45p.

SPECTRUM

NEWSPAPERS

Living without The $unday Times

Earlier this year when the *Sunday Times* raised its price to 18p many people, faced by the increased cost, were forced to face Sunday morning without it. The saving is considerable (over £7 per annum) but for some addicts the process of learning to do without the *Sunday Times* has been painful.

Jill Twombly is 42 and her struggle to come to terms with her new Sunday life-style is typical of many in recent weeks.

"Well, it was very hard at first," says Jill, a mother of two and part time media situation research assistant. "Sunday seemed empty. Ordinarily I would have spent most of the morning dawdling through the different sections trying to find something interesting. I suppose it was just a habit really. I don't miss it now. In fact, if I'm at a friend's house and see it lying around I've no compulsion to pick it up. I find I'm much happier without it. I feel fitter for one thing and of course I spend much more time with the children."

"Giving it up was no problem to me," says Keith Foggis, a dental assistant from Australia. "I said 'Right! 18p! That's it, matey!' and since then I've done without. It's had no detrimental effect in any way. I pity people who can sit around all Sunday reading that drivel."

What to do on Sunday:

Make a Chinese Kite. Two large poles and an electric blanket are ideal. Just nail them all together and throw them up in the air.

National Matchbox Museum. (Princes Risborough). Over 10 million matchboxes from all over the world (closed Sat & Sun).

Are they related?

Dr Miller **Dr Who**

Dear Old Sods.

My son Terry, 6, noticed a striking resemblance between the new Dr Who and my own favourite piece of beefcake, National Theatre director, Dr Jonathan Miller. Is there any connection? They both are doctors, and behave in a way which is out of this world.

Yours
Beryl Weembs
19 Crossett St.
Havant, Hants

■ Smart gal, Beryl, they are one and the same. Dr Jonathan Miller is feeling the pinch like all of us, and has returned to his old profession as a clown.

"What I like about this place is that it's completely unspoiled"

"Oh no, he's running a 'Football Special' again."

Whoosh! It's B.R's Super Ticket

by Our Locomotion Correspondent

A taste of things to come! This was the way British Rail described their new Advanced Passenger Ticket which will come into service in the near future.

Passengers and pressmen who arrived at Paddington yesterday were given a special preview of British Rail's New Super Ticket of Tomorrow.

Express

Said a spokesman: 'This ticket is more expensive than anything we've ever dreamed of. It's a major breakthrough for British Rail travellers. No other country has a ticket anywhere near as costly as this.'

For yesterday's experimental run the sleek slimline ticket was not up to its maximum price. When it finally comes into operation it will cost even more than it did yesterday.

And the passenger reaction?

'I think it is incredible,' said lifelong rail enthusiast Victor Mallard, 43. 'This ticket is streets ahead of anything on the continent. Iver (Bucks) for £150 – it brings a whole new dimension to the rail travelling situation at this moment in time.'

Reginald Bosanquet
News at Ten
Bristol (Parkway).

Medical Forum

Navel Fluff

by 'A Doctor'

Most people have probably experienced at one time or other the condition which we doctors call 'navel fluff', or, to give it its proper title, *microfollicosis.*

What happens is that the patient accumulates tiny particles of fibrous matter, normally as a result of his or her clothing rubbing against the perimeter of the abdominal nexus.

Normally the 'fluff' can be extracted painlessly with the help of a small brush or a pair of tweezers, and this can be done, without any risk, by the patient himself.

But there are cases, admittedly rare, when the patient is caused mental stress and in such circumstances it is advisable to seek professional medical opinion.

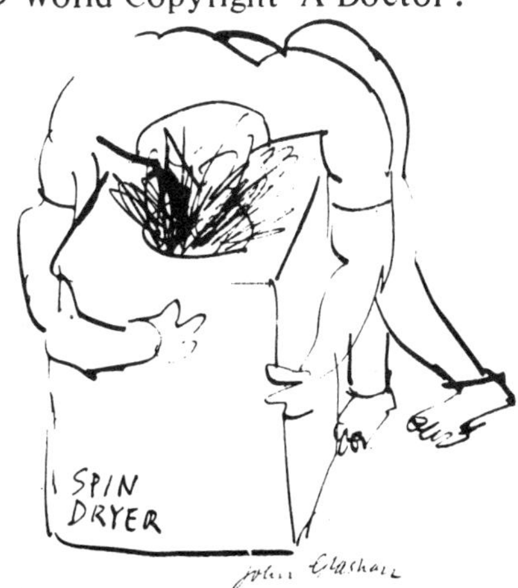

1

2

3
ALL ENGLAND KARATE CHAMPION

4
Nº1 KUNG FU MASTER

5
WORLD PROFESSIONAL WRESTLING CHAMPION

6
McLACHLAN

BBC TV

Cockeye in Limoges

For the first time ever in living memory, David Cockeye, who at 23 has become the most celebrated British painter in the world, talks openly and frankly about his work, his hopes, his fears, his laundry, his friends and his cat to Mervyn Barg.

BARG (for it is he): David Cockeye is a legend in his lifetime. When he was only fifteen he painted his now world famous satirical masterpiece 'Packet of McVities Biscuits', which won first prize at the Monty Finniston Secondary School Art Exhibition in 1955. From that point, Cockeye's rise to fame reads like a fairy tale: a retrospective show in Marseilles, a one-man exhibition in Algiers, the only English painter to be represented at La Grande Salon des Pseuds in 1962 — he seems to have said it all and he is still only 23, the age at which Michelangelo was halfway to becoming 46. On both sides of the Atlantic, Hackney is a by-word for the chic aristocrats of The New Realist School — but he himself has never followed any fashion and remains a unique figure in the world of contemporary culture.

(Ballet music from Erik Satie's 'Carnaval Bizarre'. Cut to Barg talking to Hoxted sitting in front of large canvas)

BARG: David Cockney, a lot of your pictures are of naked men in swimming pools. Is there anything particularly significant about this, do you think?

COCKEYE: Hullo Sailor! *(Giggles)*

BARG: (Embarrassed laughter)

THE END

Queen sees Japan's Industrial Might

by Anton Walbrook

The Queen today visited the vast Phuwatascorcha Industrial Complex as part of her State Visit to Japan.

She watched with evident interest as teams of Japanese technicians assembled a fully operational Plastic Beaker Disposal Unit in record time, for export to the UK.

Kung Fu

Meanwhile the Duke of Edinburgh attended a special performance of the traditional Kabuki puppet theatre.

The Duke expressed considerable interest for several hours as the story of a Zen fisherman and his love for a beautiful young flower-arranger unfolded to the accompaniment of Yamaha glass bells.

"Pretty ghastly, isn't it?" joked the Duke. "Where's the Gents?"

Emperor Hirohito is 109.

The Good News Guide

THE DAILY TELEGRAPH

Fleet Street, EC4.
Mon — Sat.
Closed Christmas/Easter.
No coloureds.

CHRISTOPHER DRIVEL

Bill Deedes took over the running of the *Telegraph* a few months ago, and it's comforting to report that he has wisely decided to keep it as it always has been. Bill – 'a diffident sort of bloke' (as one inspector puts it) – spent many years preparing the Peterborough so he knows his onions and is unlikely to institute any major changes. The fare remains solid and there's plenty of it. Saucy court reports are dished up in Gargantuan helpings – 'I couldn't finish my Lucky Lucan. I felt really bloated after two columns,' says one customer. Above all, in these inflationary days, the *Telegraph* still provides exceptional value – for 7p you get, on an average day, 32 pages which include as much news as you want combed from literally all over the world, a Garland ('rather erratic', according to one inspector), sensible arts coverage ('not too many pseuds') and the exceptional Peter Simple. Alongside all this, you have to be prepared to put up with some really appallingly done leaders, and letters which are frankly a disgrace, with little or no thought put into them. The obituaries are very poor and there's no attempt to be comprehensive. 'Thank God! No unpleasant porn!' one grateful inspector trumpeted.

App: Sir Roderick Glossop, A.J. Tharg, Maureen Clucker, Jennifer Wheatcroft.

I think women's LIB is a load of rubbish...
Let's face it, women don't make good poets, painters, disc jockeys COIN DEALERS, window sash repairers...
Do they, now?
KARAT-A TAT
Action RE-DRAW
John Glashan

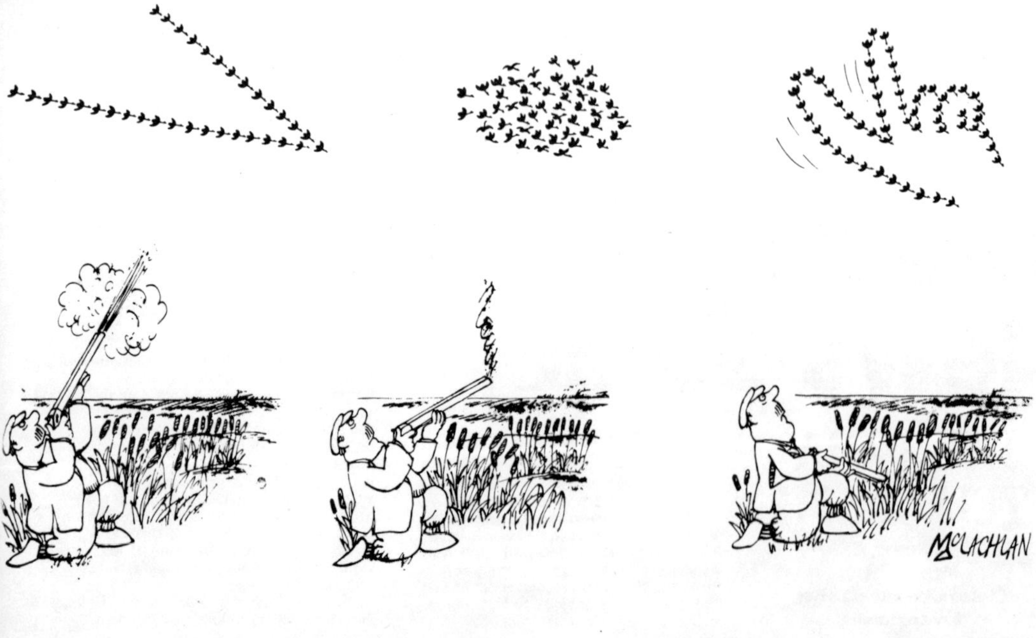

McLACHLAN

The Good News Guide

CHRISTOPHER DRIVEL

33 Holborn EC1
Tel. 01-353 0246
Mon – Sat

Older members still recall with nostalgia the great days of the *Mirror*. The fare was simple and straightforward – if somewhat monotonous. The speciality was of course the (almost) unforgettable Cassandra – pungent and salty – somehow it epitomised the spirit of Hugh Cudlipp's down-to-earth establishment. Hugh himself lent a lot of atmosphere, bluff, Welsh, and hard-drinking, he always seemed to be able to produce something out of nothing. Members even now talk about the 'Don't be so bloody rude, Mr K' which he served up in 1960.

Unfortunately we have to report that the *Mirror* has lost much of its appeal in recent years. Cudlipp has retired and the present chef-de-cuisine M. Christiansen is, as one member puts it, 'an uninspired choice'. Since Rupert Murdoch set up house across the road a few years ago, the *Mirror* has done its best to keep up with its new competitor but, alas, this has entailed an all-round lowering of standards.

Members complain of sagging nudes – 'not up to scratch'; overdone Waterhouse ('mine was very wet and I couldn't finish it' says one member); 'the Proops was old and scraggy and just made me feel sick'.

Others mentioned 'Donald Zec – simply disgusting' and 'Paul Callan – re-hashed and stale'. The only bright spot on the menu is the Fosdyke Saga, a tripe speciality which has been universally praised by members. The price is high considering the poor quality and recent disputes in the kitchen have resulted in the place being closed, in some cases for weeks on end. Keep us informed, please.

App: Roger Nargs, Basil Boothroyd, Reginald Bosanquet, Ariana Wotalotigot.

A RICH WOG

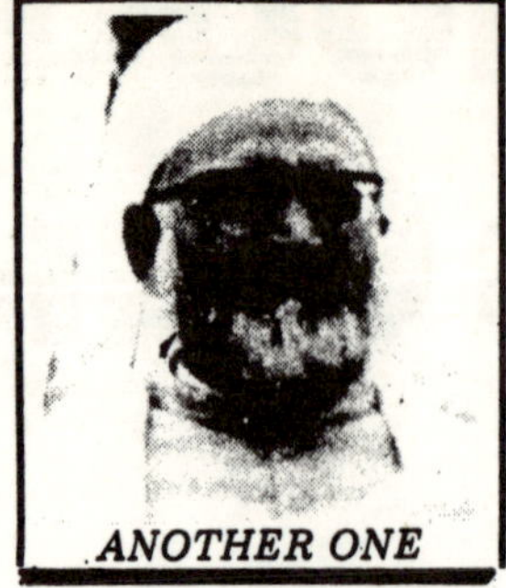
ANOTHER ONE

A THIRD

THE NEW ELITE

By Our Science Team SOLLY, WALLY, MOLLY DOLLY OLLY & POLLY ZUCKERMANN

Within the last few seconds a new race of Super-men has captured the imagination of the world.

From across the desert sands, almost silently, a group of tightly-knit Arab Sheikhs has emerged as the most powerful force ever to pull the strings of international finance on the world stage.

Make no mistake. These are no Comic Opera Bedouins of the type you might see in a Hollywood extravaganza. Beneath their colourful robes, strange at first to Western Eyes, lie a steely integrity and a brilliantly intuitive financial acumen capable of manipulating millions of dollars with the casual assurance of a Chess Grand Master.

Who are they — these Men of Today who have taken the seventies by storm, and drawn to them like a powerful magnet the cream of Europe's Top Diplomats, Master Craftsmen, Art Dealers, Bond Street tailors, Whisky Salesmen, Croupiers, Nigel Dempster, Freeloaders, Merchant Bankers, Fancy-Tie Manufacturers, Lord Chalfont etc.

BEGINNING TODAY
PART I

The most fascinating man in the world

In a large empty room overlooking two million square miles of sand, Sheikh Wel Befor Yusing sits quietly behind his desk.

Every time he blinks he is four million dollars better off. This uniquely fascinating figure is typical of the new breed of 20th Century Arab rulers who are now as much a part of the jet set stream as Niarchos, Sinatra and Robert Maxwell.

Just who is he — this quiet, deceptively diffident billionaire who likes nothing better than to sit at his desk and stare out of the window?

Enigma

On his desk there is a picture of himself sitting at his desk staring out of the window. It is a clue, albeit a tentative one, to an understanding of this highly original personality who has all the charisma and charm of a Renaissance princeling.

His hobbies are: sitting at his desk, counting his money and staring out of the window.

When in London he would like to meet Robert Robinson or Reginald Bosanquet.

"How many ants do you want?"

HURRY! HURRY!

THESE PRICES CAN'T LAST FOR EVER

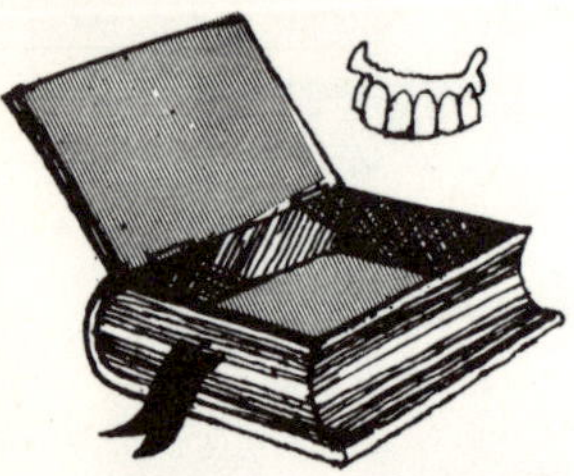

Say Goodbye to Bedtime Embarrassment with the **Denture Book Novelty.** This stylish looking 'Book' is really a handy container for your dentures. Fully waterproof. No one need ever know. Choose from these titles *War and Peace, Civilisation* by Lord Clark and *Mary Queen of Scots* by Ladv Antonia Fraser.

NEW!

A Gift to cherish.
Send £1.95 (incl.postage)

No more dog-eared L.Vs !

Thanks to the UNIQUE Luncheon Voucher TIDIVOUCH Wallet. Styled in brand new 'Leathereen' this pocket container will hold up to 6 months worth of LVs. Choice of colours: Black, office—brown and 'plain'.

Only £1.35 post free. Stamped initial service £2.50 extra.

SUPER BARGAIN!

Do you suffer from
BEDTIME BLUES?
Chase them away with

The original

HO-HO 'LAUGHING DUVET'

the Continental Quilt that actually "laughs" when you lie on it.

Makes going to bed a scream for all the family!!!

Do you remember last winter?
Don't be caught in the dark!

YOU'LL NEVER GET LOST IN THE DARK AGAIN !

thanks to these SUPER NEW CANADIAN "WELLYLITE" ELECTRIC RUBBER BOOTS.

Powered by own battery! Light your way as you walk! Fully guaranteed for THREE MONTHS!!!

Send only £1 now and nine monthly payments of £3.65.

SECRETARIES !!

Stop the TEA-SNEAK MENACE in your office NOW with a Self-Locking Cup Cap!!

With this simple device no-one can drink your tea while you're out of the office!!

Tiny batteries keep tea hot into the bargain!!

An **ideal gift** for your office colleagues. Send just **£2.99 TODAY!!**

VALUE!

MEN!

Be first with the NEW BOUFFANT HAIR Look!!

Now you too can look like famous Whampton fun personality RONALD MILHENCH in seconds!!!

- Never needs setting.
- Even the girl friend won't b able to "pull it off".
- Real simulated hair.

Only £2.50 down and five monthly payments of £6.43.

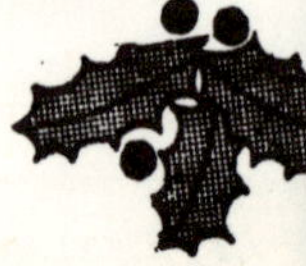

N'T MISS THIS
PORTUNITY!

SUPER BARGAINS

GRAPEFRUIT LOVERS!

NEW FROM THE ORIENT

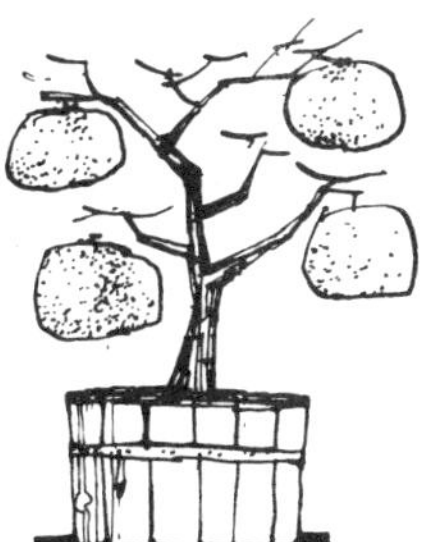

Only 6" high, this miniature grapefruit tree bears real fruit you can actually eat!! Pounds of delicious succulent home-grown grapefruit for a fraction of the normal cost. Just water and watch!

£2.25 (p&p inc.)

Do you wear GLASSES??

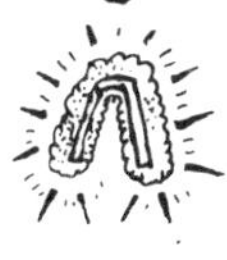

Now you can say goodbye to ice-cold specs on winter mornings!

Dr Mogg's easy-to-clip-on **Thermobridge** (US Pat. Applied For) keeps your nose nice 'n' warm from November thru' March!!

A most agreeable little device, says world-famous TV celebrity **Lord Clark.**

Optional musical extra: plays **Brando's Theme** from **The Godfather,** only £4.25 extra.

97p all inc.

Send NOW

BEAT THE SUGAR SHORTAGE AND AMUSE YOUR FRIENDS!

with the EXCLUSIVE

MUSICAL FOUNTAIN PEN ARTIFICIAL SWEETENER DISPENSER

Looks just like a luxury fountain pen costing £££s, but actually holds up to three months supply of your favourite brand of sweetener.

Just shake the "pen" into your cup of coffee and, hey presto!, it's nice 'n' sweet. And not at all "inky"!!

Make the office laugh!!!

Plays Andre Previn's **Fur Elise** Theme (as seen on TV).

£12.50 inc. V.A.T.

Beat INFLATION!!

Earn £££s in your spare time

thanks to this NEW, EASY-TO-FOLLOW LAYMAN'S GUIDE TO THE LIBEL LAWS.

Tells you just how to sue and who!

Did you know that:

- **All libel damages are TAX FREE?**
- **One man won £217,000 in a recent High Court action?**

World famous legal expert Harold Evans S.J.C.B.L. (Assoc.) explains the libel laws from A-Z (plus many easy-to-follow diagrams)

£0.99 (+ p&p).

"Every home should have one" says world-famous celebrity Arnold Goodman.

STOP PRESS SENSATION!!!

for the handyman!

Why throw away £££££s? Your old newspapers can earn

BIG MONEY

with the D.I.Y. sensation of 1974,

Home Recycler KIT

Easy-to-assemble!
Works off the mains!
Stows away in a flash!

Must be seen to be believed!!! Old newspapers vanish in seconds, producing invaluable "wood pulp waste" with a million uses!!!

Free booklet sent on request.

"Ideas like this could save Britain's economy" says world-famous industrialist SIR FRED CATHERWOOD.

+++ HURRY! +++ CANNOT REPEAT +++ NOW! +++

The twilight world of "Lucky" Longford

By Clive James Pope-Hennessy

At 4.30 on the afternoon of June 3rd, a rusty bicycle belonging to the eighteenth Earl of Longford was found abandoned outside the premises of Alf Masturbani Books and Mags Ltd., a second-hand bookshop in Frith Street, Soho. The Earl has not been seen since. . .

Edward Cholmondely Fitzgerald Francis Paul Johnson Dirty Mackintosh Pakenham inherited the title of "Lucky" at the age of twenty-one when a tree fell on him in Christ Church Meadow, Oxford. To his contemporaries, he seemed to have everything – dazzling good looks, a brilliant gift for repartee, and a reputation as one of the great lovers of his generation.

What then went wrong? His closest friends find it hard to reconcile the dapper, bushy-haired charmer of his 'Varsity days with the shambling, furtive figure so familiar to the strip-club "barkers" of London's vice world. One of them, pretty Kidderminster housewife Mary Whitehouse gave her version over a glass of Babycham in the Blue Parakeet Fun Lounge and Skittle World, Solihull.

"I think that in an earlier age, Lucky would have gone straight to the top. That, in a way, was what rankled. He knew he could have been of service, and he was born and brought up in a class whose members in the past had started the Great Fire of London, sunk the Titanic, and so forth. He felt himself to be out of place in a so-called democratic age, when being an Earl was a positive disadvantage."

Another close friend is fashionable Moors Murderer Ian Brady. Relaxing over a frame of heraldic mail-bag embroidery in his starkly furnished closed-plan living area at Parkhurst on the Isle of Wight, Brady describes how Longford would often "drop in", uninvited, for a chat:

"Lucky was getting more and more upset about the way things were going. He felt, I suppose, in his rather touching, old-fasnioned way, that he stood alone against a tide of barbarism."

Longford's friends were few, but intensely loyal. One of them, Lord "Fatty" Goodman-Shand, sometimes known as "Two Dinners" in gambling circles, where he carries considerable weight, says: "You could call it a one-man campaign, really. But in the end it became an obsession with him. He used to go to these film clubs, and would think nothing of spending a tenner a morning on books. His way of life just wouldn't support it."

Ron Muggeridge, doorman at Sidgwick & Jackson's, the old-fashioned publishers' office where Longford used to fritter away the afternoons, remembers now the ritual of Lucky Longford's day: "I recall the time Sir Charles Forte brought him in here first. A pathetic sight he was, but I suppose the idea was that he would bring a bit of class to the place. Since then it was regular as clockwork. Half past three old Lucky would roll up in his dirty mac with a bundle of mucky books under his arm. Of course he never did anything when he got in there. Just sat behind the desk looking elegant, eating dry biscuits out of a paper bag or fiddling with his rosary. We all thought he was a loonie, frankly."

© World Copyright Michael Holroyd Trustees and the Arts Council 1975.

Radio

It's Your Line to George Gale

CALLER: *Hullo, Mr Gale! I see in the paper that Media-Resources Officers in the G.L.C. are to be paid £16,500 a year. . . hullo?*

GALE: . . . *Yes, I'm listening. . .*

CALLER: *I mean, what I mean to say is, do you think it's right that, at a time when we are being asked to pull in our belts and, you know, there are millions of people in a redundancy situation. . .*

GALE: . . . *yes, yes, what are you asking?*

CALLER: *Well, it's obvious Mr Gale, I mean all these people came over here, didn't they, and I've got nothing against them personally, but frankly it's like the chicken and the egg, isn't it?*

GALE . . . *yes, well, er, it's er. . .*

CALLER: *I mean my house is worth practically nothing, Mr Gale, and when you see MPs and people getting thousands of pounds. . . I mean, this butter mountain in France. . . I mean old age pensioners can't, you know. . .*

GALE . . . *well, thank you very much for calling. . .*

CALLER: *Thank* you *Mr Gale, it's been a pleasure to talk to you.*

B.R. acts to stamp out Breakfast Horror

by Our Travel Correspondent RALPH MALLARD C.B.E.

British Rail announced shock measures today to stamp out once and for all what a spokesman described as 'the ever increasing menace of people eating breakfast'.

As from tomorrow the price of a British Rail 'English-style breakfast' (grapefruit segments, egg, sausage, bacon, fried bread, tomato *or* haddock, pot of tea (2 pers.)) is to be increased to a staggering £38.12p. + VAT.

Bacon VAT

The aim is to deter passengers from eating breakfast altogether.

Said the spokesman: 'The public ought to see what we have to deal with day after day, week after week. It is unbelievable. Particles of food all over the floor, coffee stains on the table cloth, and plates covered in bacon grease and in a filthy state. Many of them have to be washed before they can be used again. It is rough justice but we have no alternative.'

William Davis

Last year alone the cleaning-up operation after breakfast cost British Rail a record £8.3 million. The equivalent of 49 tons of bacon rind, stale rolls and unopened Trust House Forte-style 'containerettes' (as seen on TV) were removed from restaurant cars.

Bill Grundy is 52 .

BEING AN ACCOUNT OF THE LIFE AND TIMES OF THE CELEBRATED DR. JONATHAN MILLER

By his devoted friend and amanuensis

1975 **John Boswells** **AET. 41**

For these some months past I have been retired to the Scotch estates of that Maecenas of the literary arts, my Lord Lovat. It was while I was thus obscurely withdrawn from the pleasures of the world, that intelligence reached me from London of the gravest and most melancholy nature — *viz.* that my dear friend and preceptor, that Greatest Ornament to the Philosophy and Arts of our times, Dr Jonathan, had determined utterly and irrevocably to withdraw the warming light of his genius from all public concourse whatsoever.

It appeared that the great Doctor had become heartily sick of public life. For, said he, his great labours had been scantily rewarded, his genius unrecognised, and his name heaped with obloquy by a pack of envious scribblers who lacked all wit and understanding.

Conceive then of my heaviness of heart, as I revolved thoughts of that great metropolis — London — deprived forever of he who has been for so long its presiding luminary. Surely the stages must stand silent, the lecture halls must remain unattended, all vivid intellectual exchange must be at an end. It seemed as if Great Sol himself had extinguished his light, and that there was to be nothing but darkness upon the earth for ever more.

Such were my thoughts upon learning that Dr Jonathan was to become once again a mere humble sawbones in the service of the lunatiques of Bedlam, and I continued to be attended by these solemn reveries as, some weeks later I jogged southwards upon the high road to London.

Imagine then how, upon my arrival, I was struck in complete amaze to see placarded upon every wall, bills, advertisements and broadsheets proclaiming to the passer-by that my friend and his works were to be witnessed with even greater ubiquity than heretofore — to whit:

ITEM: Sir Geo. Christie's Opera House at Lewes, a production of *THE CUNNING LITTLE NIXON* by the Slavonian Frosticek — Direction of Animal Impersonations by Ye Amazinge Dr Jonathan.

ITEM: Upon Ye Stage at Greene-wiche, A Revival by Popular Requeste of Ye Olde Drama *MESMER FOR MESMER*, entirely refurbished according to the taste of the present times as a 'Freudian Case History' by ye Celebrated Savant Dr Jonathan.

ITEM: At Sir Henry Purceil's Musique Rooms, upon ye Southe Banke, *A GRAND DEMONSTRATION OF PARA-NORMAL POWERS*, being a Mysterious Discourse upon Sundrie Topicks by Ye Fabulous Doctor Jonathan, Renowned Throughout The Globe for His Eloquence, Learning and Wytte.

Etc. etc.

Upon perusal of these bills, I stepped at once to my friend's lodgings at Glos. Crescent, in order to repair our friendship without delay.

I there found the great Doctor in his accustomed chair at the centre of a rapt company, including the Rev. Nicholas Garland, the well-known moralist and engraver of mezzotints in the employ of My Lady Fartwell; Master Amis, the Infant Scribbler; Master Hitchens, a hack of Shoe Lane, and other obsequious persons.

DR JONATHAN: Why, here is Boswells, come to see us! Did I not say that he would soon weary of his native moors, and of the imbibing of usquebaugh at the hearth of My Lady Fraser?

BOSWELLS: Sir, I am overjoyed to perceive that reports of your sequestration from public view have been much exaggerated, and that society is still to be showered with the fruits of your many-sided genius!

REV. GARLAND: We so agree, Doctor!

DR JONATHAN (smiling): Why, you are right.

BOSWELLS: But tell us, sir, what concatenation of circumstances has persuaded you to put aside your earlier resolve, and to return 'so freely to the haunts of men'?

DR JONATHAN: Why, Sir, it was but a simple matter of reflection. Nature, as Dr Priestley tells us, is abhorrent of a vacuum. And to conceive of the intellectual life of the capital without my presence, is to imagine the trackless ways of Providence without the awful benefit of an All-Seeing Mind.

REV. GARLAND: Deo Gratias!

DR JONATHAN (visibly moved, and patting Rev. Garland on the head): For me to withdraw from amongst you all would be like a father who abandons his children to become hapless orphans. Why, it was something I could not contemplate — that the world should be so prematurely bereft of my genius.

At this mournful invocation, we all of us present were deeply affected and burst into sobbing. So cacophonous was the lamentation of Rev. Garland in particular that I could not but bethink myself of the howling of the forest animals in the Great Doctor's latest operatick production, when the eponymous vixen is at the last cruelly slain and the little cubs set up such a pious caterwauling as can be heard from Glynde Down to Beachy Head.

"If I was married to you, I'd divorce you!"

From the Pen that gave you LOVE IN THE SADDLE

by SYLVIE KRIN

The story of a world famous orchestral conductor — the music, the passion, the ecstasy. NOW READ ON. . .

Andre stood in the wings. From behind the black velvet curtain he could hear the muffled applause which greeted the orchestra's leader.

He waited for a moment. He made the final swift adjustments to his bow tie and shirt cuffs. Then he swept out onto the platform.

Applause as sudden, as loud as a clap of thunder roared in his ears. Like the tumultuous ocean it swept over him. It seemed to consume him, sending the adrenalin flooding through his veins like some rich dark wine.

The lights dimmed. He bowed and turned to face the Orchestra. A hush of expectancy filled the auditorium like mist on an autumn evening flooding into a sleepy valley.

In a voice audible only to the members of the orchestra, Andre murmured:

"Remember, gentlemen. Tchaikovsky's *Romeo and Juliet* is a very wonderful piece of music. It is the music of love. Let it sing from your hearts!"

Old Bob Gropes, the senior bassoonist, coughed and spat on the floor.

A nervous horn player twitched his foot involuntarily and an empty Guinness bottle rolled down the tiers of the platform and fell into a tub of geraniums.

Andre raised his baton. And then the music began. Tchaikovsky's immortal masterpiece surged out over the audience, bursting on the night air like a mighty wind.

The violins soared high above — a plangent cry of passion. The brass stuttered out a punctuation of anguish over the plaintive, beseeching oboes and the throbbing of the double basses.

And at the centre of this symphonic maelstrom stood the frail sensitive figure of Andre, his arms twisted like the branches of a tree in winter bowing before the wind.

But his thoughts were far away. Beyond Tchaikovsky's world of love and anguish. Beyond the rapturous applause of the audience. Beyond tomorrow's rhapsodic notices in the papers.

He thought only of Anna — the swinging blonde bombshell from the *Sunday Times.*

Oobopalooba! Wap! Bam! Boom!

He just couldn't wait to get to grips with that tasty hunk of Eine Kleine Nachtmusik.

From his dressing room Andre could hear the sound of the orchestra tuning up. The discordant noise seemed to mirror the turmoil within him.

Only that morning there had been yet another of those articles in the *Daily Mail.* A venomous piece of Fleet Street gossip from the pen of the most accomplished of the breed — Nigel Dempster.

Dempster. The name itself evoked images of a suave, licentious kind. The unctuous voice. The foot in the door. The power to wound beyond all measure.

With his vindictive pen this man had transformed a beautiful and pure relationship into something dirty.

Andre shuddered with distaste.

"Five more minutes, Mr Previn." The slurred tones of old Jock Dennison interrupted his train of thought:

"Best of British, maestro! You'll need it alright tonight and no mistake! The lads 'ave been round at the Two Elms celebrating old Bob Gropes' win at the dogs!"

He gave a conspiratorial wink and staggered off down the corridor.

Minutes later Andre swept out onto the platform, and was soon lost in the magic world of Sergei Rachmaninov.

As the melodies of the tortured Russian genius rose and fell Andre was transported away — far away from the seedy gossip-laden atmosphere that had enveloped him for so long.

Piccolos danced a magic scherzo high above like larks in the sky. The cellos moaned out a melody of passion.

Percussionist Arthur Weems collapsed emotionally with a crash. Harpist Gloria Trelford screamed with surprise as the tiny man slumped forward, an empty whisky bottle falling from his pocket into her lap.

On, on the music sang. From across the frozen wheat fields throbbed the age old cry of Mother Russia.

Tears flooded into Andre's eyes. His hands grasped the air. "More! More!" he sobbed in anguish. "Let it flow, gentlemen!"

A pipkin of brown ale clanged against the rostrum. A voice from the second violins shouted, "Help yourself, guv'nor!"

And then it was over. The last note echoed on the air, before the applause thundered in Andre's ears.

With his radiant face bathed in perspiration, he turned to face the audience.

It was then that he saw him — seated conspicuously in the front row — a smug grin playing about his features.

The unmistakeable figure of Nigel Dempster.

A black shadow darted across Andre's heart.

"Ten seconds!"

The floor manager looked at his watch.

"Quiet, please! We go in ten."

Andre allowed the make-up girl to adjust his fringe and dab his forehead with powder. Now he was ready to record another edition of 'Andre Introduces' for the BBC.

The orchestra were arrayed behind him. They had responded well during rehearsals.

"Good luck, gentlemen!" Andre whispered as the red light flashed on.

Smiling, he turned to face the camera.

"Good evening and a warm welcome to my Melody Go Round," he said. "Tonight we begin with one of the most beautiful melodies of Franz Schubert — his *Italian Serenade.* Schubert wrote this work during his stay in Leipzig in 1824. . ."

Clank! What was that? It sounded as though someone in the Brass section had dropped his hipflask. Andre perservered.

"I hope, Ladies and Gentlemen," he went on, "that the strains of Schubert's melodies will come back to you this evening. . ."

Crash! This time it was too loud to ignore. Andre turned just in time to see the limp form of bassoonist Bob Gropes slithering to the floor, a whisky bottle clutched in the hand that should have held his instrument.

"Cut!" the director cried.

* * *

Half an hour later, when Gropes was restored to his customary place, the music at last got under way.

For Andre, Schubert had a special place in his affections. As the music flowed he felt he was the composer himself walking in springtime through the Vienna woods, a lovely *madchen* on his arm.

Harp strings sparkled like golden corn in the sunlight. Gipsy violins played their *ziganes* as he whispered words of love to the Schone Mullerin of his dreams.

"Bravissimo, gentlemen," he purred. "Multo con brio!"

" 'Alf of lager while you're out there Bert!" yelled a voice somewhere in the violas.

The plump figure of tuba player Harry Pomfret pushed his way through the music stands with a tray of empty glasses perched dexterously above his head.

And then it was all over. The last majestic chords died away into silence. Andre felt now an inward peace within him. The peace that only great music could bring. He felt his soul resurrected.

"You're wanted on the phone, Mr Previn!" came a voice over the Tannoy. "It's a woman. She won't give her name."

Insolent titters spread through the orchestra like the first drops of a summer storm.

Eagerly he strode towards the kiosk. Who could it be? A succession of beautiful faces flashed into his mind as he took the phone.

"Hello?" he said charmingly.

"Hello nothing. This is your wife, bonehead!"

A black pit opened up and he fell headlong into a reverie of despair

---

"There were four & twenty virgins
Came down from Inverness. . . "

The raucous voices of the members of the London Symphony Orchestra filled the hot and sweaty interior of the luxury coach as it sped on its way towards Osaka.

Andre looked gloomily out of the window at mile after mile of paddy fields and tiny Bonsai pine trees growing by the wayside.

Another tour. Another month living out of a suitcase, sharing his life with the forty men who were now swaying unsteadily in their seats as they sang:

"Roll me over
In the clover. . . "

Still, Andre felt, being away from home had its compensations. Japan, after

all, was traditionally the home of many exotic pleasures. And there would be the opportunity to make new friends — to meet young people — people who would share his love of Great Music.

As the coach drew into the car park of the Osaka Hilton, Old Bob Gropes the bassoonist lurched forward and was violently sick in the gangway.

Andre shuddered with distaste.

* * * * *

That evening, bathed and dressed in his evening clothes, Andre felt revived. The sordid scenes that had marked their arrival were forgotten.

The music he had chosen to conduct — Vaughan Williams' famous *Pastoral Rhapsody* — especially fitted his mood.

From the first note he felt transported to the far away world of his adopted homeland. As the plaintive oboe sang out its plangent melody Andre was back once more in the wooded lanes of Esher, on either side of him the cornfields gently swaying in the evening breeze.

"This is the genius of Vaughan Williams, gentlemen," he had told the orchestra at rehearsal. "Search out your souls for its mystery!"

They had reached the *lento ma non troppo*. The strings fluttered tremolando like larks in the blue sky above the ripe wooden murmur of the 'cellos.

Andre felt a choking of emotion as the distant horns wistfully mourned the passing of the day.

But what was this?

Andre checked his score. There was no choral part, he was sure . And yet, he could hear voices singing, quite distinctly now, the words clearly audible:

> "*Four and twenty virgins*
> *Came down from Inverness. . .* "

Despair flooded over him, and the moment of ecstasy passed away as quickly as it had come.

Yes. They were on tour.

All the tickets had been sold months in advance. Sviatoslav Bolokhov, the great Russian pianist, was giving his only London performance of the season.

Andre, standing outside the Festival Hall, looked proudly at the poster which bore both their names in large black letters.

And Smirnov's great B Flat Concerto! It would undoubtedly be an evening to cherish and remember.

The rehearsals had gone well. Bolokhov, small and powerfully built with a bristling beard, was renowned for his quiet air of introspection. But there had been moments during the afternoon when his mood had changed and a charming smile had softened his fierce Slavic features.

The orchestra too had been on their best behaviour.

A voice interrupted his reverie:

"So vunderful to be in London, maestro!"

It was Bolokhov, emerging from the Stage Door accompanied by a group of players including the irrepressible bassoonist Bob Gropes.

"Your good comrades have so generously agreed the sights to show me!" cried the great virtuoso. "Buckingham Tower! Waterloo Square! And then tonight I shall make music to remember!"

Andre felt a thrill. Tonight! He and Bolokhov before a glittering audience! A chance for him to show the critics what he could do.

"You will join us, yes?" Bolokhov beamed. But Andre declined. He wanted to rest and check the score until he was note-perfect.

He watched the group pile into a taxi; and noticed a heavy bulging object in Gropes' pocket.

* * *

The Orchestral introduction to the Smirnov concerto is a long one. The pianist must wait a full five minutes before he plays his first dazzling arpeggio.

Andre could see Bolokhov in the corner of his vision. He sat quite motionless, his eyes closed in rapt concentration, his expression terrifyingly intense as Smirnov's immortal melodies pulsated towards their first climax.

Andre drove the music onward and still the impassive figure sat like a statue, his arms hanging limply at his side.

"Only five bars before he enters," thought Andre, "and he shows no signs of nerves!"

"Pianissimo!" he whispered. The notes of the orchestra died away in tremulous anticipation. All eyes were fixed on Bolokhov.

His arms still hanging limply, the great virtuoso slumped onto the keyboard with a horrendous crash.

Bob Gropes sniggered behind his music stand as a tell-tale bottle of Haig's, now empty, clattered to the floor from the pocket of the Russian's tail-coat.

The humiliation was more than Andre could bear and he rushed headlong from the platform.

The clock on the studio wall showed five. It had been a hard day's rehearsal. Now at long last they were ready to make the final recording.

Andre had always been drawn to Modern Music. It was he who had commissioned the widely acclaimed Scandinavian composer Lundqvist Halgrimmson to write his *Nexus Five*, especially for the London Symphony Orchestra.

It was an almost impossible piece, demanding superhuman concentration from the players.

Indeed, Halgrimmson himself had been doubtful whether it could be performed at all.

Added to the complexities of the score there was the problem of where to place the microphones so that they would pick up every tiny pianissimo fragment of the music's Nordic atmosphere.

Above all, there were Halgrimmson's famous silences — long pauses between the notes of which one critic had written: "Halgrimmson's silences are like trolls tiptoeing across the ice of his native fjords".

Andre looked anxiously at the producer framed behind the glass barrier. He had precisely half an hour in which to perform and record this masterpiece of 20th Century music.

Tomorrow he and the orchestra were due in Los Angeles to start a six month tour, and they were already "into over-time".

It was now or never.

* * * * *

The red recording light flashed on. Andre lifted his baton. A muted violin whined an icy wail like a wounded gull. The percussionist thrashed out a sudden, shocking roll on the Chinese blocks.

Andre was transported into the eerie hinterland of Lundqvist's inner musical world.

He forgot the men in front of him, with furrowed brows straining over their instruments.

He felt overcome by the magnitude of the event. This great pioneering work, dedicated to him, was being captured for ever by the modern miracle of electronic recording.

Then, at last, it was over. An almost audible sigh of relief went up from the orchestra. Behind the glass partition the producer smiled and held his thumb erect to indicate success.

* * * * *

Now the players had packed their instruments and gone. Andre waited tensely while the recording engineer wound the spool of tape back to the beginning.

"A wonderful achievement Mr Previn, if I may say so," he said. "And I think you will find that from a technical point of view it can't be faulted. These little beauties" — he pointed to the huge net-work of equipment — "pick up every-thing!"

He pressed a button. Andre eased himself back in his comfortable swivel chair. He could relax now and enjoy the music.

And there it was. The violin. The drum. Yes, it was good. He smiled the smile of a contented man.

But wait! What was that noise? Quite distant behind the pianissimo harp arpeggios!

It sounded just like a cork popping. And there! An unmistakeable glug-glug-glug!

A look of horror spread across the technician's face. "I can't understand it, maestro!" he stammered. "It sounds just like someone pouring out a drink."

Andre thrust his head into his hands. He felt the will to live ebb away. A dream lay shattered. A priceless masterpiece reduced in a few seconds to a worthless reel of tape.

Andre eased his Alfa Romeo into the fast lane and soon he was touching 80, speeding towards the metropolis.

Behind him were his wife and family. He had to admit to himself that it was a relief to get away. Mia had been in one of her difficult moods all day, relapsing on occasion into the sort of language she had picked up during her relationship with Frank Sinatra.

And, as much as he loved working with the LSO, it was a fact that he exper-ienced considerable tension during their sessions together. It was therefore all the more of a pleasure to be heading for the Ronnie Hobbs Club, Britain's Mecca of Jazz in the heart of Soho.

Jazz. The very word set his heart beat-ing faster. His mind flooded with child-hood memories — the Oswald Hickson Collier Band stomping through the night in Old Joss Bindman's cellar in 42nd Street! The dusky long-limbed ladies shimmying to the hot sounds of Biglips Dvorak on slide horn!

It was a far cry from the Festival Hall and from that handful of demanding musicians who drained away so much beer as well as all his energy.

* * *

The Ronnie Hobbs Club was packed when Andre entered. Ronnie himself, a slight bearded figure in horn-rimmed glasses greeted him with an outstretched hand.

"Hello, man! Good to see you! Glad you could make it."

He escorted Andre behind the bandstand on which an attractive blonde in a low-backed sequinned gown was crooning the Arnie Goodman evergreen, *Gray's Inn Road Blues*, through a blue haze of smoke.

When the song had finished amid a smattering of applause and a clinking of glasses, Ronnie Hobbs sprang nimbly into the spotlight.

"Well, cats!" he beamed. "I'm very proud to welcome one of the greatest all-round entertainers in music today who's come along to give us a taste of his hot piano. But before Andre begins his set I'd like to say a special thank-you to those players in the combo who've stepped in at very short notice to replace the boys who've gone down with 'flu. La—dies and Gentlemen" — the drummer began a roll on the snare — "I give you the Andre Previn Allstars!"

A brassy chorus of *Tiger Rag* drowned the applause as Andre, smiling with relaxation, picked his way across the platform to the piano.

He flicked his fingers in an up-tempo beat and strummed a riff with his left hand.

"Take it away, boys!" he murmured. "Let it rip!"

It was then that he noticed the man with the tenor saxophone lurching unsteadily to the frenzied rhythm of the stomp — beside his stand a tell-tale pipkin of Jubilee Special Barley Ale.

The name on his instrument case told the whole story — R. GROPES.

Suddenly the music stopped swinging for Andre.

"Of course, you're more than welcome to stay the night"

One person's week

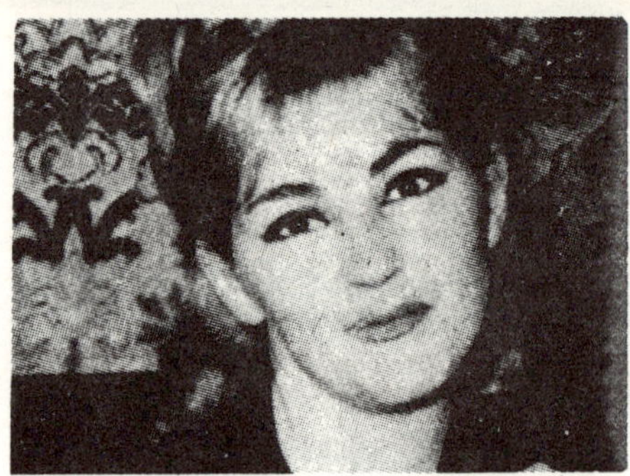

By WENDY SHAGG

Wendy Shagg, 23, came down from Cambridge last year after reading ***The Lord of the Rings*** *at a typing school. Now a freelance journalist, she writes regularly for the* ***New Statesman*** *and has appeared on several Melvyn Barg book programmes.*

Monday

Usual bloody post-week-end hangover again. Spent the morning trying to get rid of some bloke I'd met at a party. I really hate Monday mornings.

Begin to think about my *New Statesman* piece on comprehensive schools in Gateshead. Who'd want to live in bloody Gateshead, for Chrissake?

Tuesday

Lunch with Chris Trott and Claire Tumbelin from the *NS.* We go to this really unspeakably grotty Indian restaurant in Gerrard Street. Why is it that waiters in Indian restaurants can't speak English properly? Chris tells a very good dirty joke about the Irishman whose wife wouldn't go on the Pill. I can't remember the punchline because we were all a bit pissed by that time!

Wednesday

Tony Howard rings up to say he doesn't want the comprehensive schools piece after all – could I do something on devolution by tomorrow. Put on Heavy Sausage and smoke a joint hoping for inspiration.

Thursday

Take round my piece on devolution which I am sure is the best thing ever written on this boring subject. In the evening I go off to a really fantastic dinner party at Martin Amis's. I look round the table and think: "Zowie! These are all the most interesting, exciting, fantastic people in London today!" They are all in the media, and all incredibly successful. There is Chris Trott, Martin himself of course, who has just written this fantastic novel called *Dead Vomit,* Claire T., Tina Barg (who is a fantastic new talent in various media), Belle ffrench-Lettres, who is married to Jonathan Bumblebee, the amazing new pop group who are going to put Heavy Sausage out of business. There is also a little man in a motor-cycle jacket who seems very pleased to have been invited, and says he is the editor of the *Sunday Times.* He offers me a 'slot' on his back page to write about anything I like. He is very sweet and keeps on saying in a groovy Northern accent, " 'appen. Life's a challenge, like". We all get fantastically pissed.

Friday

Usual bloody pre-week-end hangover. I go off for late lunch at Vermicelli's. Usual crowd there – Martin Walker, Hardy Amis, Chris Fenton, Belle ffrench-Lettres etc. We all get completely smashed.

I think: "This will make a fantastic entry for One Person's Week which I am sure all those tedious little zeroes who read the *Sunday Times* in places like Gateshead will find absolutely riveting".

LIFESPAN

ECO CORNER by Geoffrey Wheatgerm

As eco-catastrophe nears, and the total exhaustion of fossil fuels grows increasingly imminent, more and more people are trying to become totally self-sufficient in ecological terms. Only last week Lord Ross and Cromarty, who owns an 800,000 acre estate in Sutherlandshire, appeared on the BBC's *Man Alive* TV programme, showing how he and his family have managed to survive for a whole year simply on the pheasants, venison and other produce of his 23 farms. But even if you live in a bed-sitter in Earls Court, you too can play your part in building up an autonomous life-support system. Many people recently, for instance, have turned to growing mustard and cress as a relatively cheap means of garnishing their fillet steaks (with bags of rich, life-giving vitamins into the bargain!).

Bake your own Bread, then lie in it.

Many of my readers have written in asking for instructions on how to bake their own bread. Certainly shop-bread is one of the great killers of modern society, according to a recent article in *The Ecologist*. So all the more reason to join with the thousands of bio-dynamically minded people who are joining the 'Dough It Yourself' movement every day!

What you knead!

It is absolutely vital that you get the right ingredients. These are:

Hand-ground, organically compost-grown, whole germ, stone-milled flour. This can be obtained only from Karl and Jonathan (Millers) Ltd., The Auld Granary, Peebles, at £28 for a 2 kilogram sack.

Yeast is what bread is all about. Again, only pure, organic, whole-germ, fresh, live, Eco-Yeast will really do the trick. Obtainable from the W.B. Yeast Co., Isle of Innisfree, Co. Galway, Eire (£5.75 a 2oz portion, inc. VAT).

Water – this is the real secret of a perfect loaf. Did you know that a cup of ordinary tap water contains enough chemicals to poison an Eskimo (see last week's *The World About Us*)? Only pure, organic, whole-germ spring water is suitable. Obtainable from Elsie and Doris (Waters) Ltd., The Auld Dykes, Llandrindod Wells, Brecon. £5 a bottle, plus £2.50 for p&p.

Last (but not yeast, as we old hands say!) comes **salt**. Ordinary shop-salt contains enough impurities and chemicals to poison the entire *World In Action* team. Pure, organic, whole-germ sea salt (hand-evaporated by Yemeni tribesmen in goatskin *panhs* – see last week's *Horizon*) can be obtained from Salt of the Earth, Walton-on-Thames, at only £87.50 for an airtight tin.

NEXT WEEK: How to recycle your old yoghourt pots into low-tar, organic herbal tobacco (see this week's *Blue Peter*).

OBSERVER REVIEW

MICHAEL FRAYN'S

NEASDEN

An article of the type which David Astor is appealing to the nation to preserve.

SUNDAY morning in Tesco Road. The sky is an unbroken grey. All over Neasden, the sound of ten thousand transistors, tuning up. *'I loved you yesterday, baby, but tomorrow is another day. So-o-o please don't go away'.* The words waft ironically upwards from a hundred once-laburnum-lined avenues, as the Neasdenians prepare for the weekly ritual of *carwascherei.*

A soft drizzle begins to blunt the edges of reality. Inside the bus-shelter I meet a young student, Rolf Spart. He has the raw, shifty look of a typical young Neasdenian. He tells me his father works in the VAT office in Attlee Avenue. Rolf is sardonically ironic about life in present-day Neasden. 'If I had the bread, man, I'd emigrate to Sardinia', he says sardonically. 'I do not want to end up as a VAT-man, like my dad.'

I Ron Knee

Neasden wears its historical heritage lightly. It is hard to believe that ten years ago, the suburb still

contained a number of buildings which dated back to the Second World War. Today, all that is gone. In its place, the new Neasden of housing estates, shopping precincts and pedestrian underpasses looks at the world with an oddly sardonic air. Wittgenstein says: 'If we look in a mirror, we must be careful if we do not wish to be deceived'. How ironic is this comment from the *Tractatus* when set against the atmosphere of one of Neasden's traditional *bierhausen.* In the saloon bar of The Spitfire Arms I discussed Wittgenstein with a locally-born VAT official. 'He was a good horse,' he said with an ironic shrug, 'should have won the 2,000 Guineas'. Such misunderstandings are typical of Neasden's traditional *tomfoolerei.*

I walk through the empty streets, still heavy with the stale, pungent smell of last night's *fischundchipperei.* A solitary wanderer is turning in beneath the dirty plastic sign which proclaims 'MONTY GERHARDI – NEWSAGENTS AND TOBACCONISTS. A.J. Patel Prop.' He asks, in his thick Neasden slur, for the *Sunday Times.* Mr Patel gives a typically ironic shrug. 'All gone! Sorry mister'. His customer looks temporarily confused. 'Alright then, mate. Gimme the *Observer* and 10 Silk Cut'. In the street, he carefully unfolds his paper, and takes out the review section. His lips move slowly as he deciphers the headline 'Living In The Past – Michael Frayn Visits Vienna'. Methodically, and with a savage irony, he squeezes it into a ball and throws it into the gutter. A passing dog sniffs it, and lifts an ironic leg.

"It was . . . AAAAAAAGGGGGGGHHHHH. . . ."

"George Herbert AAAAAAGGGGGGGHHHHH?
We have reason to believe. . . . ."

GASKET'S

RURAL RIDES

Boston to Nairn

July 2nd. Set off today along the A796B (M) Porchester-Staines Flyover and stopped for a hearty breakfast at Grotley Hill Moto-Snackery Services (chips beans and sausage £1.80. Terrific value and only waited half an hour in the queue). While I was about it, I took the opportunity, as the old tank was getting dryish, of filling up with their 4 Star Super-Plus. I branched off down the BO496 where you can really put your foot down, only to find that just north of Byfleet the warning light was blinking away and it was time to top up again.

Typical, thought I, of this modern mass-produced juice we are forced to fill up with! Luckily for the motorist who still appreciates his petrol there are still a few places in the country left where you can buy the juice straight out of the can. I chanced upon such a spot – Nargby, Notts. – home of Chesterton's Very Strong Petrol, a really heavy old-fashioned brand with a rich aroma and a very slight rose-pink tinge to it. A pint of that in your tank is worth a gallon of the gassy modern rubbish the big boys knock out by the tanker-load. (*Andover Casualty Tent*).

TV

Face the Morons

Cooper: Hullo again. Hahaha. And tonight my guests are Robin Ray . .
Ray: Hahahahahaha!
Cooper: . . . Hahaha! Rita Chevrolet . .
Chevrolet: Mozart, isn't it?
Cooper: Hahaha and Sir Alec Douglas Home.
Home: Haha!
Cooper: We begin with our Upside Down Composer when we play a famous Symphony backwards on an ocarina — that's a tiny wind instrument, in case you didn't know - hahaha
Robin Ray: Ho ho ho.
Cooper: . . . and our panel have to guess what the composer had for break-fast. Off we go hahaha.
(Silent film of Paderewski addressing the Polish Chamber of Commerce)
Cooper: Robin?
Ray: Hahahaha. You always give me the hard ones.
Chevrolet: Beethoven innit?
Cooper: Hahaha. I'll give you a clue. This is a hard one to UNRAVEL.
Ray: Hahahahahaha.
Sir Alec: Zzzzzzzzzzz!
Cooper: And now for our underwater opera (*Contd. Channel 94*).

£10,000 plus

Appointments Vacant

Neasden Borough Council requires a

Community Kinship Research Officer

Applicants need have no experience or qualifications (although a degree in Sociology is preferred).

The Community Kinship Research Officer will be required to head a project team to locate potential stress-situations involving areas of emotional deprivation among problem families, and to implement a long-term environmental amelioration programme across a broad range of social strata.

£14,650 p.a. Full pension rights.

Newport Pagnell District Council seeks applicants for the post of

Assistant Refuse Clearance Officer

This interesting and varied job will involve the successful applicant in regular travel, the use of up-to-date technological aids and communicating with a wide cross-section of the public in their home environment. He or she need have no professional qualifications, although experienced dustmen will be preferred.

£11,680 p.a. Hours 8-12, four days a week. Full pension rights.

Dollis Hill Borough Council seeks

Principal Senior Asst. Director of Leisure

The London Borough of Dollis Hill requires a fully-experienced Leisure Administrator to plan and supervise the installation of its proposed indoor hang-gliding leisure project. This will be the largest of its type in the country (estimated to cost £20 million) and is intended to become an international centre for indoor hang-gliding championships. The applicant is expected to be able to read and write.

Salary £34,612 p.a., in addition to which the job carries a 6-bedroom house, 12 weeks holiday, full pension rights, luncheon vouchers and a life peerage.

HOW FAR HAVE YOU GOT?

Perhaps you haven't noticed — but Britain is in the middle of an exciting new revolution! Make no mistake — metrication is going to change all our lives in ways most of you can't even imagine!

We at the Metrication Board have been working away around the clock for years — making sure that metrication when it comes will be just as easy and painless as possible.

But, you know, soon life's going to get pretty difficult for those of you who don't or won't play the metrication game.

> "Just remember, a metre
> Is not the same as a litre"
> says Mr Metrication.
> SIMPLE, ISN'T IT?

For example, it won't be any good you going into a shop and asking for "half a pound of butter". Most likely the shop assistant will just look blankly at you — while fellow customers will fall about laughing.

Or again, it won't be much use stopping your car and asking "how many miles to the nearest pub, where I can buy a pint?" You'll probably get run in!

> "Acres into hectares?
> That's just fine!
> You multiply by 0.339"
> — says Mr Metrication.
> SIMPLE, ISN'T IT?

Don't misunderstand us. We can't force you to go metric in the privacy of your own home.

But, you know, if you insist on talking about feet and yards, you'll soon find the neighbours are beginning to talk!

Very soon, even your best friends will be avoiding you. Your family will cease to look up to you. Your private life will be exposed by Nigel Dempster. Your hair will begin to fall out. You will go blind. Bull-dozers will mysteriously demolish your house during the night hours. Psychiatric tests show that you will almost certainly undergo a John Stonehouse-style breakdown.

> "A half-pound of jam
> Is 0.56732 of a kilo-
> gramme!"
> — says Mr Metrication
> SIMPLE, ISN'T IT?

Important

We must emphasise that metrication is entirely voluntary. That's why there's never been an Act of Parliament about it.

But unless we all join in, there's no point is there?

That's why we're hoping that, from 1 June 1976, it will be a criminal offence to use non-metric measures in public, even in conversation. This offence will be punishable by imprisonment or a fine of £1,000 or both.

GOVERNMENT HEALTH WARNING

Metrication can cause blindness

The Good News Guide

200 Grays Inn Rd. Tel. 837-1234 Mon-Sat. (Closed Christmas Day, Good Friday and in event of staff disputes.) Readers 900,000. Moggs allowed, if on lead.

This is the first time this world-famous old establishment has appeared in the guide since its move to new premises (specially designed by the notorious Col. Seifert) in somewhat unfashionable north Holborn. Not so long ago, members will recall, *The Times* was still the bastion of traditional British fare, cooked and served in time-honoured way by a staff of octogenarians. Back in the swinging sixties, Canadian-born Roy Thomson, helped by his friend Dennis (the Brigadier, as he is known to regulars) tried to give the place a new look, by jazzing up the menu and encouraging pot-smoking in the newly-opened Mick Jagger Room, but a lot of members found the changes too drastic. Manager William Ress-Mogg ("don't, for heaven's sake, call him Bill") has now evolved a somewhat synthetic compromise between "trad" and "mod", and members must be warned that the cooking is very variable in quality. There have been many complaints all through the menu – "half-baked arts pages", "long, stodgy leaders – I just couldn't finish them", "special supplements – totally indigestible, an insult to the discriminating palate".

The *Levin Supreme* is still regarded as Chef Charlie Vass's *piece de resistance*, but again many members have complained that it is "highly unreliable". "Some days it is very good" writes one inspector, "but several I have sampled recently were simply drenched in *schmaltz*, truffles, Wagner and conceits of all kinds. Quite disgusting!"

In far too many respects, ***The Times*** appears to be living on its reputation. The obituaries and letters are still worth a nibble, but titbits like these do not make a newspaper. The price is exorbitant, and for real nourishment, readers are recommended to go elsewhere.

App. R.T., W. R-M., B.L., Michael Ratcliffe.

CHRISTOPHER DRIVEL

Yes, It's a Postal Service for the 80's!

by Our Communications Staff
G.P.O. THARG.

An entirely new-look postal service tailored to meet the needs of the last quarter of the 20th century, was unveiled today by Sir William Rys-Mogg, head of the Post Office Corporation.

OUT GO – old-style letters, telegrams and phone calls. "After all, these things were invented in the Victorian era" quipped Sir William.

IN COME – millions of postmen sitting round doing nothing and being paid £100 a week.

Shock

Under Sir William's scheme, which has been introduced to meet Mr Healey's plan to make nationalised industries "economically viable", the letter and telephone service are to be "phased out" over the next three years, by putting up prices until no one can afford them, except Mr Paul Getty and Mr Sidney Weighell.

Nobel Prize for incompetence

A top British Official is among those named today among the winners of this year's Nobel Prizes.

He is Sir William Ryland, 56, Chairman of the GPO.

Triumph

In the citation, Sir William is described as having "advanced the frontiers of bungling ineptitude to hitherto inconceivable limits".

His discovery, this year, in his London office, of the 8½p stamp, was "only the climax to years of administrative vandalism that would leave humanity immeasurably impoverished".

Breakthrough

When I spoke to him on the telephone yesterday, Sir William was surprised to hear the news.

"I haven't heard anything about that," he said. "I think there may have been some mistake. Nobél – how are you spelling that? Are you sure you haven't got a crossed line? Hello?"

I asked Sir William if he would travel to Stockholm to receive the award in person.

"Stockholm, you say: that is in Africa, isn't it? I am not sure if I can give a firm answer at this moment in time. Not at least without consulting my secretary. Just hold on, I'll give her a buzz. Hello, Mrs Hetherington? What day is it today? I've got someone on the internal line I think it is who says I am going to Stockholm. Just hold on Mrs Hetherington, I'll ask him. Hello? Are you still there? Mrs Hetherington was just wondering what the date would be for the prize-giving. I know I can't manage Wednesday, because I have got to go out to Raynes Park I think it is to have a dekko at our new £8,000,000 filing and retrieval unit with the automatic Venetian Blinds. And I think Thursday is out because that's the day some of us at the top of the nationalised industries have a meeting with the Prime Minister to lodge a formal protest over the non-implementation of the Boyle recommendations, I've got them here somewhere on my desk, which would have given us a massive (contd. P. 94)

Peter Jay talks to Professor Eduardo Luni, author of 'The Human Carburettor' and Reader of Applied Kinetics at the University of Tristan da Cunha.

JAY: Professor, in your book you postulate – or as I interpret it – you appear to be saying, or at any rate writing, that – the passage to which I am referring occurs, I think I am right in saying – I am sure you will recall it – in Chapter 47 where, if you remember, you attempt to analyse – in a way which I personally, and I am sure many other people, find or will find very helpful – the whole problem of what we may call, to use your own categorisation, 'conceptualisation modes'. Now, I know that we are here straying into the whole, very difficult area of epistemology, but what I would like to put to you is this – let us assume, for the sake of argument, that, if we predict. . . (contd. p. 94).

Norris short-listed for Canterbury

By Our Religious Affairs Correspondent CLIFFORD LONGFORD

The race for Canterbury is on! And the hot favourite, given 5–4 on by Ladbroke's last night, is the Ven. Reginald Bore-Gooth, at present Suffragan Bishop of Combe Florey.

Bore-Gooth, 51, took a brilliant second in Divinity at Auckland University in 1922, and rowed bow for the Caius College 3rd VIII in "Bumpers" in 1929. He is a broad-shouldered extrovert, keen on pipe-smoking, sherry and "meeting young people".

Also well up with the leaders is Rev. Ronald Bore-Tharg, 51, the present Bishop of Gibraltar and All the Isles. Bore-Tharg is a bluff, no-nonsense extrovert, who has won a large popular following for his series "Hey You Out There" on Grampian TV. Bore-Tharg is a dedicated pipe-smoker, admits a fondness for sherry, and thinks that "the greatest challenge facing the Church today is getting across to young people". He saw Godspell three times and was, in his own words, "very very moved".

There is a growing feeling in the Church, however, that it is time for the Anglican Communion to make a meaningful gesture to groups hitherto unrepresented in the Church's leadership.

Many younger churchmen are calling for the appointment of the first coloured Archbishop. If so, a front-runner must be the Very Rev. Jomo Mbogo-Nthargi, 51, Bishop of Mogga Mogga. Mbogo-Nthargi, who took a distinguished degree in Forestry at the University of Lesotho in 1931, is keen on rugger, sherry and "meetin' de young folks". When in London he would like to see Godspell, and meet Eric Morley, Chairman of Mecca Dancing.

There is also an outside chance that the Church may make a really imaginative gesture by picking its first woman archbishop. The likeliest contender is Deaconess Gladys Boothby-Norris, 51. Miss Norris, who was captain of the England women's cricket XI on the Australian tour of 1952-3, is Chairman of the Church of England Advisory Council on the Harmful Effects of Sherry Drinking and Pipe Smoking on Middle-Aged Clergymen. She also has a strong dislike of young people, and while in London she would like to meet Mr. Reginald Bosanquet.

Deaconess Boothby-Norris is 51.

GOODMAN LASHES 'FAT, GREEDY LAWYERS'

'Only interested in money'

Saint's indignant outburst

THE BLESSED Arnold Goodman today hit out at "a tiny minority among his fellow-members of the legal profession, who, he claimed, "are only interested in making enormous piles of money".

Lord Goodman spoke with passion of "hugely corpulent, heavy-jowled figures" sitting in "plush offices off the Strand", and terrifying their clients by sending in "gigantic bills which bear no relation to the services rendered."

Lord Goodman is 94 stone.

APR/RRI

4 Little Essex Street
London WC2

E. Strobes Esq.
Gnome House.
London W1

22 October 1974

In account with

Goodman Derrick & Co.

Re: Damage to bumper of vehicle reg.no. ARG 001N

		Charges and disbursements
September 19th 1974	*To professional services* in relation to the above matter, viz. listening to your telephone call describing an alleged incident in Tesco Road, Neasden, on October 1st 1961; to making notes on same; to forgetting matter entirely for three weeks; to listening to your further instructions enquiring why the hell I had done nothing about the matter; to making feeble excuses during the course of said conversation; to passing whole matter on to articled clerk, viz Michael Tharg; to said M. Tharg writing a professional letter to you requesting further and better particulars of the said matter; to having said letter typed by professionally qualified person, viz Miss Janice Brocklebank-Fowler; to folding, sealing, and stamping of letter; to making carbon copy of letter for filing purposes; to consulting London Telephone Directory to ascertain your full and proper place of abode; to the taking of the aforementioned letter down three flights of stairs, and along street to a proper place of despatch as ordained by the Postmaster General, viz a pillar box; to waiting four days for receipt of your reply; to full and due perusal of your letter of 7th instant; to taking cognizance of the contents thereof, and in particular your suggestion that ourselves had shown "gross incompetence and idleness" in pursuing this matter, and in noting your instruction to us all severally and collectively to take a running jump into a duly specified place, viz one lake. We herewith take pleasure in rendering our full and final account in the sum of	£8,984. 68 + V.A.T. £726. 42
September 20th 1974	P.S. Further to the above, we beg to render the following additional account in respect of this matter, viz to typing of above bill, to perusal of same, to correction of typing errors with Rubinstein's Patent Eraser, to licking of stamp on envelope, and to rubbing of hands at the thought of enormous cheque in the post.	£461. 34
October 20th 1974	P.P.S. We beg to inform you that owing to the incidence of inflation since we began the compilation of the above bill, the total liability now amounts to	£25,468. 00
	N.B. We further beg to inform you that failure to render settlement in full within 24 hours will result in our placing the matter in the hands of our legal advisers, Messrs Goodman, Derrick & Co. "MONEY IS OUR BUSINESS"	

A bill of the type to which it is believed Lord Goodman strongly objects.

RELIGIOUS AFFAIRS

Only 23% believe in 'Contract'

by Our Religious Correspondent DOMINIC MINTOFF

Only 23% of the population now believe in the existence of the Social Contract.

That is the gloomy conclusion of a special poll conducted for Private Eye by Gnome Polls Ltd.

SAD

But the poll suggests that there are a large number of people (73%) who, though not believing in the Social Contract *per se*, do nevertheless accept that there is a mysterious "something out there" which they cannot fully understand.

Only 8% are prepared to say that the contract "definitely does not exist and was invented as a trick to fool people".

Despite the widespread scepticism about the contract, however, the majority of people (81%) now think that even though it may not exist, belief in it is all the same "a good thing" and "helps men and women to live better lives in the context of the community as a whole."

Michael Foot is 83.

BBC2 Wednesday 8.30

They were tough, those days, and they made 'em tough. The men of Barnsley were made of iron, like the ships they built. Starting this week, famous Northern playwright Alan Bennett recreates all the toughness of those days in a new series – *'Appen, Life's A Challenge Like* – which tells the story of how one tough Northern family, the Parkinsons, battled for survival. David Pryce-Jones needed some money and agreed to write this awful article introducing the series.

Ee ba goom, 'appen

"I've tried to tell it like it was," says famous playwright Arnold Bennett, himself a Barnsley man. " 'Twere tough in those days, sweetie, and no mistaking like."

Bennett has long been fascinated by the Barnsley milieu of the '20s and '30s, in which the hero of his new series, Michael Parkinson, grew up.

"It was a world of trams, cobbled streets and jam butties," he says. "Today it's all Chinese take-aways and high-rise flats, but in those days, when Parky was just a barefoot lad in clogs waiting outside t'mill, they knew how to live."

In the twenty-five parts of his series, Bennett traces the dramatic rise to fame of Michael Parkinson, from his humble beginnings as a mitten-darner's son in Tripe Street to fame and fortune via the new medium of television.

In the early episodes, in which period atmosphere is lovingly re-created down to the last Gold Flake cigarette, we meet a host of larger-than-life characters.

There's old "Granfer" Parkinson, the tyrannical, Bible-thumping retired dripping-stirrer, who lords it over Tripe Street with a rod of iron. There's Margaret Drabble, the severe young schoolmistress, who shows her soft spot for young Parky during Sunday School at the local Baptist Tabernacle. There's bustling, ambitious young 'Oonter Davies, cub reporter on the *Barnsley Enquirer,* whose life's dream is one day to write about men's underwear in a national colour supplement.

But above all, there's Parky himself mop-haired, backward at his books, mad about cricket and collecting cigarette cards. There is a moving episode early in the series where the young cricket-fan is taken by his "Granfer" to Bramall Lane to see Neville Cardus asleep in the press-box while Emmett Robinson is taking all day to score four runs in a classic "Roses Match" of the 20s.

For the young Parky it was a Damascus-style experience. From that moment on, he was determined that one day he too would open the batting with Ronnie Corbett and David Frost in a Charity match at Sittingbourne, Kent, in aid of Distressed Comedians.

As young Parky grows up, it is not long before Barnsley becomes too small to hold his burning ambition. He decides to leave for London, and there is an angry scene (which viewers will see next Boxing Day) when "Granfer" rounds on him:

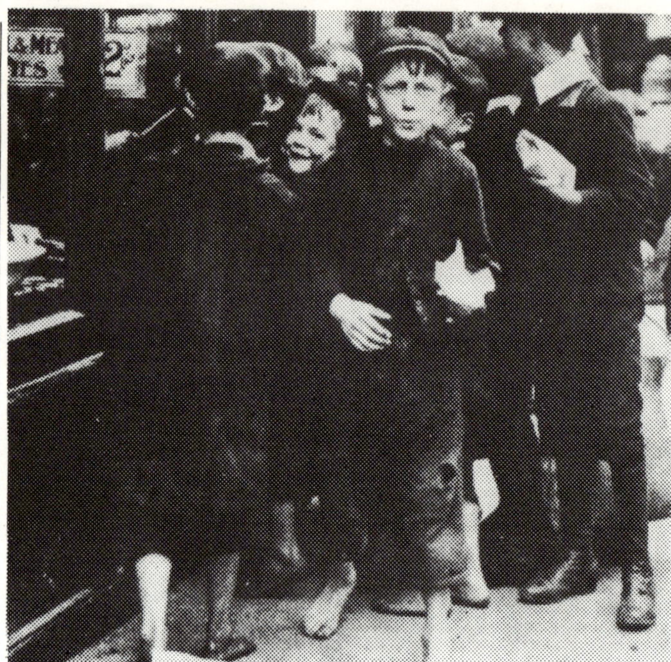

Young Parky as he appears in Episode One

"So Barnsley isn't good enough for the likes of thee, lad? Who does thou think thou art, our Mike, all dolled up like an an Heyetalian ponce? So thee wants to get down to London to interview Mahomet Allah and the like – well, goah then, y'bugger. But don't gang rahnd hyar agen, y'auld pooftah!"

It is a sign of scriptwriter Bennett's marvellous perfectionism that he spent over eight months in researching the dialect for this passage, by tape-recording the conversations of more than 2,000 disc-jockeys.

From then on, Parky's rise to fame is fast and furious. Scarcely has he stepped off the train at King's Cross than he is signed up by the dynamic, talent-spotting editor of the *Sunday Times*, Frank Giles, and becomes the most famous sports journalist of all time.

He marries a beautiful girl and buys a 36-room Thames-side mansion. Within months he is given his own TV show, interviewing famous personalities. And finally he passes into legend when, in a deeply moving scene, he agrees to have his brain cut out in front of an audience of millions. The operation is a complete success, and Parky is able to carry on just as before. Not even his wife notices the difference. ●

CAST (in order of appearance)

Young Parky.	MELVYN BARG
Gran'fer Parky . . .	EMMANUEL SHINWELL
Gran'ma Parky.	RENEE SHORT
Michael Parkinson	DAME HAROLD EVANS
Frank Giles	BILL GRUNDY
Neville Cardus . . .	WILFRED HYDE-WHITE
Margaret Drabble	JOAN BAKEWELL
Mary Parkinson.	ESTHER RANTZEN
Fred Yobbo	FREDDIE TRUMAN
Georgie Best.	ANDRE PREVIN
Man in Taxi	DAVID FROST
Brain Surgeon	JAMES ROBERTSON-JUSTICE
Man in Underpants . . .	'OONTER DAVIES

Theme Music "Life's A Challenge Like" by Frank Schon and Harry Kissin, played by the Birtwhistle Silver Works Band.

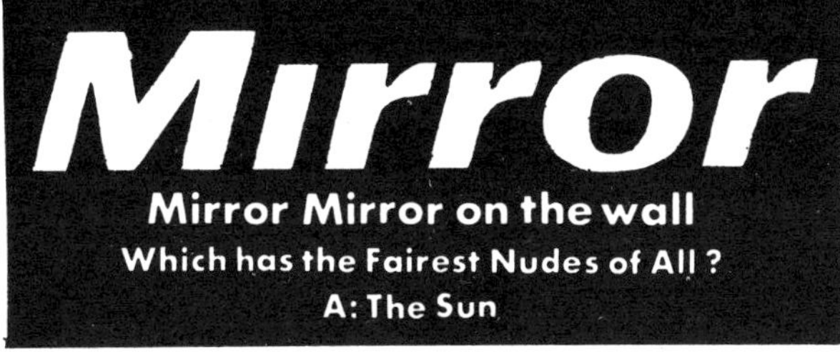

SNOW WHITE

"It must not happen again"

Verdict

'IT IS UPON SOCIETY AS A WHOLE THAT THE ULTIMATE BLAME MUST REST'

ACTION will be taken by the Government to ensure that the shocking story of Snow White will never be repeated.

Last night an eight million page report by a panel of 73 experts called for drastic changes in the laws concerning adoption, fostering, and the whole complex system of administration with regard to all aspects of child care.

BLAME

Social Services Secretary Barbara Castle will today commit the Government to drastic new laws which will prevent any repetition of the Snow White shock horror drama etc.

She said: "Every man, woman and child in Fairyland is responsible for this appalling breakdown in our child-care system. We should hang our heads in shame that this can happen in 1974."

EMOTIONAL

The report singles out for special censure the notorious "seven men of restricted growth" who obtained custody of the little girl.

These men, the committee states, had had no training in the techniques of child maintenance and should never have been allowed to supervise Snow White's welfare.

As a result of their "culpable negligence" the child's step-mother gained illegal access to the dwarves' dwelling and administered a fatal dose of poisoned apple to the little girl.

TRAGIC

It was clearly shown that the seven dwarves were in the habit of going out early in the morning whistling and singing, leaving the child alone and unattended for long periods of time. During the day Snow White was used by the dwarves to perform domestic duties without any

SNOW WHITE

financial reimbursement.

Subsequent investigations have uncovered the fact that at least one dwarf, known simply as Dopey, suffered from "a personality defect" as a result of which he became a state-registered drug addict.

DOPEY: "Defect"

CRIMINAL

But the report reserves its severest censure for officials of the Children's Welfare Department of the Enchanted Forest Rural District Council who are guilty of what the experts term "a failure to monitor the progress of Snow White during the period she was in the dwarves' care."

INFORMATION VACUUM

The N.S.P.C.C. is also criticised for ignoring "an area of potential social distress". The Society, says the report, did not react meaningfully in a situation which contained factors of possibly far-reaching complexity."

WHAT THE MIRROR SAYS page 2

ROYAL DIVORCE SOUVENIR SUPPLEMENT

Tony & Margaret

HOW THEY PARTED

by KENNETH ROSE-BARING, The Man Who Knows More About The Royal Family Than They Do Themselves.

✫ It was the Fairy-Tale Separation of the century! How every married woman's heart must have beat a little faster when she heard that Her Royal Highness the Princess Margaret and the Earl of Snowdon were to part!

To foreigners it was an object lesson to show how the British can still stage these great Events of State better than any other country in the world.

HOW IT ALL BEGAN

The story of how the Princess and the Photographer came to hate each other's guts goes back much further than many people realise.

Friends who know the couple intimately first began to notice that all was not well between the Royal pair as long ago as 1963.

Intimates like Francis Wyndham and Derek Hart recall the unmistakeable signs at exclusive Kensington Palace soirees: "He used to give her those *looks*," says Wyndham, "and the *way* they used to talk to each other — you could tell that something was up, mmmm!"

Before long, friends noticed that Margaret and Tony were always apart. It was impossible to keep them together. And on the rare occasions when they were in the same room, they just couldn't keep their hands off each other — as they fought, kicked and scratched. "Just like a pair of rhinoceroses," affectionately recalls another Kensington Palace habitue, Jocelyn Stevens.

For a long time the secret was as closely guarded as any in the land. But it couldn't be kept dark for ever.

Godfrey Winn

One sunny Spring morning, as the first daffodils peeped out through the frosty sods of St James's Park, the nation was told the news.

Church bells didn't ring out. Old age pensioners stayed at home dying of hypothermia. Britain received the solemn announcement with a stony indifference.

Two weeks later the country held its breath as, amid the hushed solemnity of a solicitor's office in the heart of London, the venerable figure of Britain's first Primate Lord Goodmanzee, pronounced the hallowed words that were to seal the separation of the unhappy pair for all eternity:

"That will be 5,000 guineas, Ma'am. My clerk will look after the details."

ODE ON THE SOLEMN SEPARATION OF H.R.H. PRINCESS MARGARET AND THE EARL OF SNOWDON, BY THE POET LAUREATE, SIR JOHN BETJEPERSON.

Gosh, oh dear! What jolly bad luck!
Poor old Tony, and Margaret too.
Their nuptial bliss has come unstuck,
It seems the 'arrangement' has fallen through.

I wonder what Brenda will have to say,
Back in the Palace over tea.
I expect there'll be all hell to pay,
I'm jolly glad it isn't me!

Poor little kiddies, off to Bedales —
Who's going to tell them, will it be Granny?
It might be their uncle, the Prince of Wales,
Or dear old Crawfie, the Royal Nanny!

On the 8.15 from Sidcup and Slough,
There's only one topic of conversation.
Who will they both get off with now?
At least, it makes a change from inflation!

Cheerio, old beans!
J.B.

WHO WILL SUCCEED

by Our Form Correspondent, MAGNUS CARTER-RUCK.

✫ So Lord Snowdon bows out — after 15 turbulent years holding down what has been described as "the most gruelling job in Britain" — being married to Princess Margaret.

Who is likely to succeed him? Already a host of eager contenders have thrown their hats into the ring.

These are the chief rivals so far in what has been described as the 'race of the century'.

A clear favourite must be the "caretaker" candidate — Roddy Llewellyn. Youth is on his side, and his strong family connections with horses must endear him to his prospective sister-in-law. "He has much in common with the Princess," quipped one punster. Against him, however, must be set his long hair and muddy boots.

Next, as the darling of the media, is the dapper Derek Hart-Throbbe, a onetime TV personality. Hart-Throbbe seems to fit the bill admirably, being only three feet in height (slightly shorter than the Princess). On the other hand, he is very middle-class and this might stand out on State occasions.

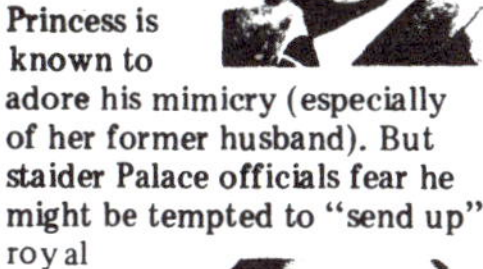

Peter Sellers. At least there'd be no money problems here! The Princess is known to adore his mimicry (especially of her former husband). But staider Palace officials fear he might be tempted to "send up" royal functions.

Making a strong late bid is former Prime Minister, Ted Heath. In his favour — the fact that he is unemployed and has never been married before. He would therefore be no embarrassment to the Queen in her role as Head of the Church. Against him, however, is his difficulty in speaking "the Queen's English", which he pronounces with a strong foreign accent, like the late Duke of Gloucester.

RODDY & YVONNE

A SYLVIE KRIN SPECIAL

As the burning scarlet ball of the tropical sun sank into the purple haze of the ocean, Margaret stepped out onto the terrace.

A soft sea breeze ruffled her thin silk evening gown. The night air pulsated with the whirr of the *picardas*, while down on the beach she could hear the distant throbbing of the famous Monty Finniston and his All-Steel Band.

Mustique! The very word itself spelt "Freedom". Freedom from the glare of the public eye, the pompous state occasions and the million other cares of life as a Princess.

The scent of bougainvillea wafted up from the gardens. Why tonight? Why did she feel a sense of burning expectancy in the hot tropical night?

By now the moon was full in the sky, bathing the whole island in a silvery glow.

Suddenly she realised that she was no longer alone. On the beach below, she could see a figure silhouetted against the gently shimmering waves. He was coming towards her!

A young man, almost naked — his tousled hair lapping his shoulders, the muscles of his well-tanned body rippling easily in the moonlight.

Margaret caught her breath.

"Who can it be?" she thought, as the vibrato of the *picardas* throbbed ever louder in the darkness.

Was it a lone native fisherman, returning to his hut? Donald Crowhurst? John Stonehouse? 'Lucky' Lucan looking for a bridge-partner?

Nearer and nearer drew the figure. The tension was unbearable.

And then he was standing before her.

"Good evening, lady," he slurred. "The name's Gropes, Principal Bassoonist, L.S.O. Call me Bob. We were playing on this cruise ship when — I don't remember much about it — but somehow I found myself in the drink, so to speak! By the way, have you got an opener? I seem to be holding this bottle of lager."

A dark cloud drifted across the moon. The Princess's dreams lay shattered in a million fragments.

THE END

HERE AT LAST!
THE PUBLISHING EVENT OF THE YEAR!
You Can Forget Hornblower — The Cruel Sea — Moby Dick — Captain Pugwash — IT'S ALL HERE!

Never before has life on the ocean wave been captured so vividly between two covers! The tang of the spray comes off the pages of this book like a Force 10 Nor-Nor-Easter!

The creak of the rigging, the flap of the sail, the groan of the rowlocks — they're all here, etched with a master pen!

As one critic, "Jock" McCosgrove of *Yachting Fortnightly* puts it: "After only a few paragraphs, I wanted to don my oilskins and sou'wester. Never before has any author captured so magnificently the mew of the gull, the rattle of the anchorchain, and the slap, slap of the 'sheet along the yard'. Make no mistake, this book is an immortal epic of the sea."

Now for the first time Private Eye *is proud to present a first exclusive extract from*

Edward Heath's

"Hullo Sailor"

(to be published next week by Longford Books, £89)

PART I
HOW IT ALL BEGAN

Everyone should have a hobby of some sort, to provide him with relaxation in his leisure time. For me, sailing has become my main leisure activity. I find that, once on board, I can forget all about the day-to-day problems of my political career.

There is always a lot to keep you busy on a boat. Just as in politics, careful preparation is the key to success. Before setting sail, you must make sure of certain basic requisites.

The mast is an important factor. So are the sails. Without mast or sails, sailing would be little pleasure!

I am sometimes asked, what sort of clothes should a man wear to go sailing?

Well, something waterproof is clearly a first priority! It can sometimes get pretty wet out there, and so can you!

PART 2
WHAT I THINK OF WOMEN SAILORS

In recent years, more and more women have come to the top in all walks of life.

I am often asked, "Could a woman skipper a winning crew in the Hobart-Tasmania race?"

Well I never, what a ridiculous thought! Just imagine a woman at the helm, for heaven's sake!

© World Copyright Dametrash Productions 1975

[As Told To Michael Parkinson]

INVESTORS!

UNIQUE Richard BURTON OFFER

Gnome Very Wonderful Silversmiths Ltd are very proud to offer you in the privacy of your own home the opportunity to take part in an entirely new investment experience.

To commemorate the 10,000th bottle of whisky drunk by Mr Richard Burton our highly skilled craftsmen (B.D. Twombly F.R.B.D.S.) have struck a limited edition of six commemorative silver-style medallions which will be hurried to you when you fill in the coupon below.

These very wonderful *objets d'art* have been acclaimed 'Medallion Masterpieces' by *Yield,* the House Journal of the Phuwatascorcha Trading Co., Rebecca West Street, Osaka, Japan.

These exclusive items are mounted on a simulated velvet-style surround and depict in vivid detail great moments in Richard Burton's historic career as a world-famous piss-artist.

Only ten sets of these epoch-making medallions have been minted. Each one is numbered and bears the authentic facsimile signature of maste engraver Twombly.

Our price: Only £800,000 per medallion (+VAT).

EMBRACE HISTORY TODAY.

Hurry, hurry while stocks last.

Send to:
NAME. . . . .
ADDRESS. . . . .
. . . .

Gnome Trading Co., Harpenden, Beds.

World of Art

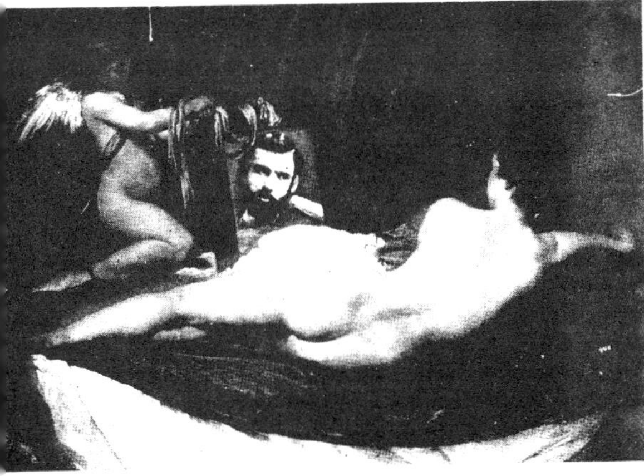

The Rokeby Venus as it will be seen

New "Non-Sexist Look" for Old Masters

by Our Saleroom Correspondent
GERALD NORMAL

More than 2,000 of the world's most famous old pictures are to come under the scrutiny of the Equal Opportunities Commission, it was announced in Manchester last night.

A special committee, headed by Lord Clark, will be asked to advise on ways in which the paintings can be 'brought into line' with the new legislation.

FACT: As from 1 January this year, it is illegal to show women in 'female role situations' such as working in the kitchen, minding the baby or posing in provocative, sexist positions, unless an equal number of men are shown in similar postures.

Lord Clark last night admitted that the task of his committee would be "very, difficult".

"But I have every hope", he said, "that within a few years we can remedy the more grossly discriminating aspects of Britain's artistic heritage."

Personet's Water Lilies

I asked Lord Clark how his Committee would proceed.

"Well," he told me, "with some pictures, it will be merely a matter of changing the title. Whistler's Mother, for instance, will simply be renamed Whistler's Parent.

"But in other really serious cases of iconographic sexism, we shall have to arrange for the whole picture to be repainted.

"Certain painters are notoriously prejudiced in this way. In the Middle Ages, for instance, it was fashionable for a lot of painters to depict a woman in a mother-and-child situation. At least half of the Madonnas by Giotto, Bellini Raphael and others will have to be restructured to show Joseph doing his share of the housework." (*Laughter*)

What of the famous "nudes", admired by art-lovers the world over? Many of these too are unmistakeably sexist, and will be replaced by carefully selected undress portraits of Mr Roy Jenkins, Lord Balogh and Mr Sidney Weighall.

Make no mistake about it — many of Britain's most familiar masterpieces will never be the same again! For a start, they will be referred to in future as personpiece

DOWN TO EARTH

LOOK!

N.W. Three Veg

A Sunday Times guide to some exciting new plants that you can really eat! by MICHAEL BEETROOT, VANESSA DRIVEL and a cast of thousands of otherwise unemployable Sunday Times hacks.

In these days of eco-doom, suddenly everyone's growing their own macrobiotic recycled food. But to make a change from all that dreary old avocado vinaigrette scene, how about trying something that's really different?

Pele Beans

(from Brazil). High in protein, although it tastes a bit like rancid yoghourt, this plant is ideal for any very sunny garden where the temperature never drops below 80°. Try it with Yugoslav goats cheese.

Purple Bigotry

(Ranunculus Purpureus). A cross between a marrow and a plum, this relative of the buttercup is a succulent herb with a bitter, tangy taste. It is deadly poisonous and should on no account be eaten.

Selfridge

Looks like a lettuce, but is rock-hard and blue in colour. It is easy to grow, but don't cook it unless you've got six weeks to spare!

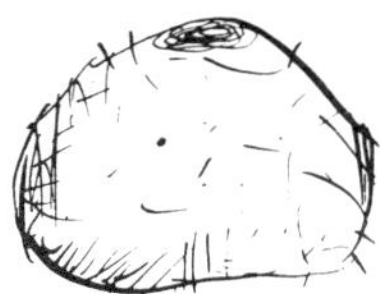

Giant Peruvian Leek

(Haroldus Evansensis Giganticus). This plant, which often grows to 100 feet high, is only recommended for the very largest garden. It likes a rich, loamy soil, and requires 50,000 gallons of water a day. Feeds 10,000.

3 old ladies locked in lavatory shock horror

Convenience siege enters sixth day

by 243 SUNDAY TIMES-MEN WITH NOTHING BETTER TO DO

Neasden, Saturday.

The great Neasden 'Lavatory Siege' has entered its sixth dramatic day with no change in the overall situation.

Inspector 'Knacker of the Yard' Knacker, who is in charge of the 4,000-man police operation, said that 'this siege is now following the classic pattern'.

Shock

This was the shock sequence of events which led up to yesterday's dramatic lack of activity:

● **Monday.** The three old ladies entered the 2′ 6″ square disused urinal in Tesco Road, Neasden, for reasons best known to themselves.

● **Monday evening.** Passers-by hear shrieks and hammering. 'We are locked in!' cry the captive trio. Within minutes, armed police have cordoned off several streets.

● **Tuesday.** Day Two. Press and TV men move in. The nation waits.

● **Wednesday.** Day Three. The world holds its breath.

● **Thursday.** Day Four. Conditions in the convenience now officially described as 'hellish'. The world holds its nose. Playing cards and copies of the *Sunday Telegraph* are dropped in to the old ladies by helicopter.

● **Friday.** Day Five. First sign of a breakthrough when one of the old ladies succeeds in passing through the door a coded message addressed to the Spanish Consul, and demanding to be flown out to an 'underdeveloped nation'.

Amazing Drama

Today Inspector Knacker told reporters: 'Frankly lads, this is an open-and-shut case. That is, the door is shut, and we want it open.'

But Scotland Yard is now hopeful of an early and peaceful ending to the 5-day drama.

Said the Inspector: 'As we might expect, the old ladies have been growing quite friendly towards each other. They have been playing bingo, with the numbers shouted in through the keyhole by some of my officers.'

STOP PRESS

4 a.m. Neasden Siege Over.

The three old ladies, trapped in a Neasden toilet since Monday, were released in the early hours of this morning.

Dismissing reports that 'nobody knew they were there', Inspector Knacker said: 'This is frankly ridiculous, to my mind. The whole world was watching the siege on TV. It has been an extremely useful exercise for my lads in rehearsing for the forthcoming collapse of civilisation.'

"I'm terribly worried I might live – !"

LORD GNOME
in association with
Abdullah Cigarettes
His Royal King-Size Holiness
MAHOMMAD L. ADOLF NARG (Shit of Persia)
Port Said Leather Pouffe Co.
(Hasim Bros. Prop.)
& Neasden Urban District Council
proudly present

A CELEBRATION OF ISLAMIC CULTURE

For centuries the master treasures of the magical world of Islam would have laid hidden in the Secret Places of Arabia.

Now for the first time we in the west are privileged to be shown these outstanding masterpieces of decorative art.

For the first time, too, we can hear the mysterious strains of Islamic Music played on authentic instruments, just as it was in the days of yore.

CARPET 493 B.C.

EXHIBITION OF VERY WONDERFUL CARPETS

G-PLAN CENTRE
TESCO ROAD

(To be opened Friday April 23rd by His Imperial Excellence WASHIN-AP-LIKWIDH, Press Secretary, Yemeni Consulate)

Scholars agree that the carpet patterns of Persia constitute one of the great climaxes of mankind's struggle to raise himself to sublime heights of art.

From the famous bazaars of Ferguskhashin Alhankoran and Djimkallakhan we have assembled for your delight a modestly-priced selection which will make your living room a palace fit for Allah himself.

NEVER TO BE REPEATED BARGAINS!

Where to go

TILE 478 B.C.

EXHIBITION OF PRICELESS ISLAMIC CERAMICS

King George V Memorial Hall
(Neasden)

Centuries before Michaelangelo the sons of the desert had created a wonderland – a veritable kaleidoscope of mystical designs.

Fortunately owing to popular public demand many of these priceless works of art can be yours – for a mere fraction of their original cost!!

These very wonderful antiquarian "Plasti-tiles can transform your bathroom into a Sultan's seraglio.

Hurry! Hurry!

HERBERT MORRISON LEISURE CENTRE.
Woolworth Road, Sunday April 29.

In the presence of His Royal Highness Lord Chalfont C.B.E.

A CONCERT OF ISLAMIC MUSIC

to be given by
Monty Boxwallah (wobbla)
Reg Mohammad al Wheatcroft (tungla)
Benny Green (alto sax)

For free illustrated brochure write
Box 97949 Welwyn Herts

McLACHLAN

New exam proposed by board

by Our Education Correspondent
Lunchtime O'Level

A totally new type of exam, replacing 'O' and 'A' Levels, University Entrance, the 11-Plus and the Driving Test, is proposed in a report published today by the Associated Board of Associated Boards Advisory Committee.

The new exam is designed to eliminate all forms of what the Board calls "divisive selectivity situations in examination situations".

Instead, candidates will be tested on the basis of "an all-round personality assessment" which will take account of such things as 'self-expression' and 'relating to other members of the community in a meaningful way'.

Typical of the kind of questions which will be put to candidates, either orally or in written form, according to choice, are:

What is your favourite pop group?

What are your out-of-school hobbies?

Are you on the Pill – and if not, why not?

When you are in London, who would you most like to meet – Michael Aspel, Dr Who, Melvyn Barg or Malcolm Allison?

Above all, says the Board, the new exam will eliminate for ever the stigma of passing or failing, which has "branded whole generations as second-class citizens".

Under the new system, all candidates who sit the exam will receive a simple certificate, to indicate that they have 'taken part in an examination situation'.

This will entitle them to free bus-fares to and from their local Employment Exchanges.

The report, *Beyond the Examination Trauma*, is published by the Associated Board of School and University Associations, in conjunction with the Department of Educashun. (*HMSO* £28)

AUTUMN BOOKS

MY DARLING BEAVERKINS – the correspondence of Lord Beaverbrook and A.J.P. Taylor. Oldbore Press. £21.

Now at last it can be told – the full inside story of a famous historian's 40 year infatuation with a disgusting old Canadian businessman. Steaming off the page as freshly as the day they were written, these torrid love letters comprise one of the frankest documents ever published. As Beatrice was to Dante, as Eloise was to Abelard, so was the relationship between the shy but passionate don and the wrinkled entrepreneur.

'Absolutely marvellous and enthralling. This is history as it *should* be written.'

Lady Magnesia Freelove,
Evening Standard.

EGG, SAUSAGE AND CHIPS TWICE – the Virginia Woolf Cookery Book: edited and compiled by Michael Holroyd and Robert Gathorne-Sailor. Limited edition. Hogarth Press. £120.

It is a little known fact that, when she died, Virginia Woolf left behind an incomparable collection of old recipes, jotted down on the back of cigarette packets. 25 of these have now been painstakingly assembled, and are published for the first time, on Japanese vellum, with a specially-written introduction by Michael Holroyd. Four engravings based on original etchings by Roger Fryup. Foreword by Dr Roy Strange.

'Virginia was never really much of a

cook,' writes Lord David Cecil in his poignant postcript, 'and this book helps to explain why.'

Also published this week

NO WAY – the A.A. Book of Cul-de-Sacs. With introduction by Graham Hill and a Foreword by H.R.H. The Duke of Edinburgh. Readers Digest Publications. £11.50.

THE BUMPER BOOK OF DREAMS by the Rt. Hon. Reginald Maudling. Slumberbooks. £5.

One of the world's leading authorities points the way to deeper sleep in this new collection from his treasure-trove. By the same author: **Fat Without Worry, Jobless in Gozo** and **Dozing is My Business.** With foreword by His Imperial Holiness, the Maggithachershi of Arineavana.

Save Pounds! and Headaches with a Gnome Pocket Calculator

Say Goodbye to hours at your desk adding up yards of figures.
G.P.C. gives you the answer at once with 100% accuracy.
Just tap out the numbers and hey presto!

Accrued Dividend Mean Trend

Press Button B for money back.

Synthetic Yields Hyper-Quotient

Press 1+5+X. Then add percentage multiple 6. Tablespoon of Basil. Simmer for two mins. in Oven (Regulo 2.54 +3.6). Serve.

World War Three Advance Signal

Press Red Button for four min. warning. Run for shelter.

TL TL n TL

Your Trains Tonight

See Button 94.

Test Match Scor

India 14 for 6. Veribadbatsman 0 Nobluddigud 1 Hopliz 0 Inkrediblibhad 4 Littlebittbetha 9 n.o.

G.P.C.can do anything your brain can do ONLY A HUNDRED TIMES QUICKER.

Can it help me with V.A.T.?

Yes–and much much more besides. For example G.P.C. can sub-divide multiple co-ordinates to 8 decimal points + percentage ratios at 100 x (infinity) in less time than it takes to write it down.

How much does it cost?

Multiply £87 by 143. Then add £5,601. Add V.A.T., P&P to taste. Press the answer button. And there's your price in a flash!
+ G.P.C. also gives you
- Dates of famous battles
- Best years of Chateau-bottled claret
- Birthdays of members of the Royal Family
- Even your own I.Q. (to the nearest 8 decimal points)

HURRY HURRY Don't be disappointed. The opportunity of a lifetime. Write to:

Gnome Noveltex Co. (PE)

Harmondsworth PO Box 79694. Middx.

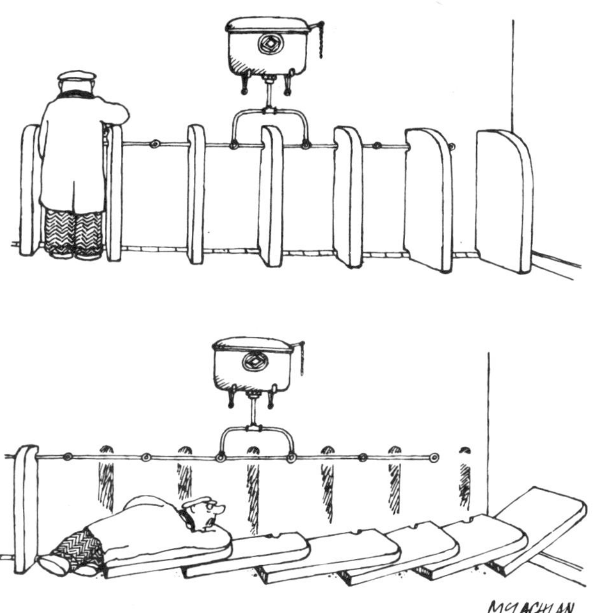

NEW SUPERDEAL FROM LEYLAND

British Leyland are proud to announce a multi-million pound super deal which affects you – you – and YOU!

We call it – The Safe One.

From tomorrow when you buy a British Leyland car we guarantee to tow it away ENTIRELY FREE OF CHARGE.

PLUS

- Take our new 'Homestead' 1000 cc *(see picture)* masterpiece of up to the minute engineering.
- Each model comes complete with the names and addresses of all the repair services within 100 miles of your home.
- Length of stout towing rope.
- Set of breakdown 'winking' lights.
- Free accomodation for one night only at the Trust House Forte hotel of your choice.

All this plus a unique British Leyland first – the Homestead.

Just look at these exciting revolutionary new features – Four Wheels (two front; two back) – Rainproof petrol tank – Hand operated steering wheel – Roadholding ability and leopard-skin accessories – PLUS (need we say it?) BIG savings on petrol.

HOMESTEAD 1000

Hurry Hurry while Stokes lasts

LEYLAND

British and proud of it